**J. TOM MORGAN**
Attorney

160 Clairemont Ave.
Suite 500
Decatur, Ga. 30030

Office:   404-687-1002
Cell:    404-218-0697
Fax:    404-373-6418

P.O. Box 1324
Decatur, Ga   30031

JTOM@JTOMMORGANLAW.COM

# IGNORANCE IS NO DEFENSE™

## A Teenager's Guide To Georgia Law

### 2008 Edition

## J.Tom Morgan

# IGNORANCE IS NO DEFENSE™
## A Teenager's Guide To Georgia Law
*2008 Edition*

By J.Tom Morgan

Published by
Westchester Legal Press
Decatur, GA

ISBN: 978-0-9796625-1-5

Library of Congress Cataloging-in-Publication Data
available upon request.

If you have questions or comments about this book, you may contact J.Tom at jtom@ignoranceisnodefense.com

www.ignoranceisnodefense.com

*Design and layout by Glennon Design Group (www.glennondesigngroup.com)*

This book is dedicated
to my children
Caroline and John

# ACKNOWLEDGMENTS

I am grateful for the love and support of my wife, Carol, who inspired me to complete my law school education over 25 years ago. I am also deeply appreciative of the valuable insights and editing provided for this book by the following people: my wife, Carol; our children, Caroline and John, whose writing talents constantly inspire me; our niece, Laurel Parker, who has the wisdom and perspective of a former high school teacher and recent law school graduate; my mother, Virginia Morgan, who patiently endured my teenage years; my legal assistant, Joanne Mayer, who typed the original manuscript; and my respected colleague and former Chief Assistant of the DeKalb County District Attorney's Office, John Petrey, and his son, Daniel Petrey, who is also a recent law school graduate.

---

### TO ORDER THIS BOOK:
Fax or send your purchase order to:
Westchester Legal Press
P.O. Box 1324
Decatur, GA 30031
Fax: (678) 732-9348
### OR
Purchase online at www.ignoranceisnodefense.com
### OR
Call: (678) 732-9348

### FOR SPEAKING ENGAGEMENTS:
Contact J.Tom Morgan at jtom@ignoranceisnodefense.com

# TABLE OF CONTENTS

## PART I: FUNDAMENTALS

# PART II: WHAT'S THE CRIME?

## DRUGS AND ALCOHOL

## *SEX CRIMES*

## PART III: EXTRA STUFF

# PART I: FUNDAMENTALS

# INTRODUCTION

MY INSPIRATION FOR THIS BOOK comes from working with thousands of youth throughout my career. As a prosecutor for many years, I prosecuted young people who violated the law. I also helped young people who were victims of abuse and prosecuted the abusers. I worked with high school students as a church youth group advisor. I have spoken to many groups of high school students about laws affecting teenagers and listened to their stories. As a private attorney, I defend teenagers who are in trouble with the law.

I have seen a lot, and I have heard a lot, about teenagers who violate the law or who are hurt by others who violate the law. I want to give teenagers the tools to avoid these circumstances.

What I enjoy most about teenagers – their questioning minds and fun-loving spirits – are the qualities that sometimes lead to trouble. Many teenagers stumble into trouble without fully comprehending the law and its consequences. From my experience, teenagers almost never intend to do something hurtful; their acts are often just plain stupid.

Because "ignorance is no defense" to a violation of law, our legal profession has a duty to ensure that teenagers (and parents) are informed about the law. With proper education and understanding, teenagers usually respect and follow the laws.

Unfortunately, teenagers also find themselves in situations where they are victims of crimes. Sometimes teenagers do not even realize that they are victims. Teenagers need to be able to recognize these situations and understand their rights.

I hope that this book will empower teenagers with knowledge about laws that affect them; enable early intervention in problem situations; and prevent problems from arising in the first place. My goal is for teenagers to lead safe, happy, and fulfilling lives – engaging their questioning minds and fun-loving spirits – without encountering the criminal justice system.

## MORE ABOUT THIS BOOK

This book describes laws in Georgia that may impact teenagers. I compiled the laws based on my experience as an attorney in the public and private sectors and included examples of situations involving these laws, many of which are based on actual cases. To protect the privacy of individuals, I have not used real names and sometimes used "Person A" or "Person B" to describe an individual in an example.

Most of the laws described in this book are criminal laws. I also discuss some non-criminal laws that may affect teenagers, such as driver's license requirements and boating laws.

Depending on the code section, Georgia law uses the terms "child," "minor," and, in some cases, "adult" to describe a person under 21 years old. The age of adult responsibility under Georgia law varies depending on the circumstances. For example, you can be prosecuted and punished as an adult for murder at age 13, but to consume alcohol, you must be 21 years old to be an adult. In this book, I usually use the term "person" with the age of the person noted where appropriate.

Chapters divide the book into common, related subjects; a glossary defines terms you need to know; and the index helps you quickly find where a law or subject is discussed in the text. If you want to read the Georgia statute relating to one of the subjects in this book, see the Appendix for a list of citations.

**The purpose of this book is to be a helpful guide to Georgia's teenagers.** This book is not intended to be a comprehensive legal treatise on Georgia's juvenile laws or criminal laws. It is also not intended to give legal advice to someone who may be in trouble with the law.

### ◀)) *Pay Attention!*
*If you are in trouble, or you know someone who is in trouble, you need to consult a lawyer.*

# CHAPTER ONE
## CRIME AND PUNISHMENT

## OVERVIEW OF CRIMES

Most people have a general idea that it is against the law to do certain bad acts, such as murder. However, many people do not know how or why certain acts are classified as crimes. A <u>crime</u> is an act of doing something that violates a written law which may be punished with imprisonment; for example, possessing marijuana is an act of doing something that violates a written law. A crime may also be the failure to do something required by written law; for example, a parent who fails to give a baby nourishment violates a written law. All crimes are defined by <u>written law</u>. Written laws are called <u>statutes</u>. Statutes are made by a governing body, such as the legislature of a state.

Most of the crimes discussed in this book are violations of Georgia state law and were made into law by the Georgia legislature. Definitions of crimes in Georgia can be found in *The Official Code of Georgia Annotated.* The United States Congress also makes laws that are criminal statutes. However, most of the laws that impact teenagers in this state are Georgia laws. This book will primarily discuss laws passed by the Georgia legislature.

This book refers to a person who commits a crime as a defendant, perpetrator, or offender. This book refers to a person against whom a crime is committed as a victim.

Just because you did not know something was a crime does not get you off the hook. *Ignorance of the law is no defense.* The fact that police officers, prosecutors, defense attorneys, and judges in this state cannot recite from memory all of the criminal laws in Georgia is not an excuse. (While researching this book, I found several laws I never knew existed, and I have been a lawyer for over 25 years!)

## ♀ *Did You Know?*

***DID YOU KNOW that passing a joint to a friend is a felony and that passing a joint to a friend on school property is a separate felony?***

### EXAMPLE

*Person A, who is 17 years old, shares a joint with a friend on school property on a summer night when school is not in session. Person A is arrested by the police and charged with two crimes: distributing marijuana (a felony with punishment of 1 to 10 years in prison) and distributing marijuana within a school safety zone (a felony with punishment up to 20 years in prison). Prior to Person A's arrest, Person A did not know that sharing a joint with a friend on school property violated two separate Georgia laws.* **Person A cannot use ignorance of the law as a defense.**

## ⚲ *Did You Know?*

**DID YOU KNOW that giving a prescription drug to a friend may be a felony?**

### EXAMPLE

*Person A has a valid prescription for Tylenol III®. While at school during a lunch break, Person A gives one Tylenol III® pill to Person B who is not feeling well. Person A is guilty of distributing a Schedule III drug, which is a felony, with punishment of 1 to 10 years in prison. Prior to Person A's arrest, Person A did not know that Tylenol III® is a Schedule III drug or that giving a Schedule III drug to another person is a felony.* **Person A cannot use ignorance of the law as a defense.**

## ⚲ *Did You Know?*

**DID YOU KNOW that you can be charged with statutory rape even if the other person tells you that he or she is 16 years old?**

### EXAMPLE

*Person A is 17 years old. Person A believes that Person B is 16 years old. Person B tells Person A that Person B is 16 years old and looks at least 16 years old. Person A has sexual intercourse with Person B. Person B is actually 15 years old. Person A is guilty of statutory rape. Prior to Person A's arrest, Person A did not know that Person A could be charged with statutory rape if Person A made an honest mistake about the other person's age.* **Person A cannot use ignorance of the law as defense.**

This book describes crimes teenagers need to know, including some of the more serious crimes and their consequences. However, do not rely solely on this book for all your knowledge of Georgia's criminal laws. If you have a question regarding whether an act is a crime, it is best to consult a lawyer.

## ◀))) *Pay Attention!*

***If you think that doing something might be a crime – don't do it. It probably is a crime, particularly if you gave it any consideration.***

If you do not think something described in this book should be a crime, or if you think the punishment does not fit the crime, then when you turn 18, elect someone to change the law. Or, better yet, get elected to the legislature and get the law changed yourself! *Do not violate the law just because you do not think something should be a crime.*

## TYPES OF CRIMES AND PUNISHMENT

A <u>felony</u> is a crime for which the punishment is more than 12 months in prison, life imprisonment, or death. In Georgia, felonies are prosecuted in superior courts by district attorney offices.

A <u>misdemeanor</u> is a crime for which the punishment is 12 months in prison or less. In Georgia, misdemeanors are prosecuted either in 1) state courts by solicitor-general offices in large counties, or 2) superior courts by district attorney offices if the county does not have a state court.

Punishment for a felony or misdemeanor may be imprisonment, probation, and/or a fine. You can learn more about different types of punishment in Chapter Seven of this book.

The state legislature determines whether a crime in Georgia is a felony or misdemeanor as well as the punishment for the crime, including whether a crime has a mandatory sentence or a specific fine.

A city or county ordinance is a law passed by the governing authority of a city or county. Violations may result in imprisonment (up to 6 months in the county jail), probation, and/or a fine.

Persons under 17 years old commit delinquent acts rather than crimes and will be prosecuted in juvenile court. An exception to this rule is if a person 13 years old or older commits one of the seven deadly sins. For these crimes, a person 13 years old or older can be prosecuted as an adult. The seven deadly sins are 1) *murder,* 2) *voluntary manslaughter,* 3) *rape,* 4) *aggravated sodomy,* 5) *aggravated child molestation,* 6) *aggravated sexual battery,* and 7) *armed robbery with a firearm.* You can learn more about prosecution as an adult for these crimes in Chapter Five of this book.

A <u>designated felony act for juvenile offenders</u> is a crime for which a person 13, 14, 15, or 16 years old can be sentenced up to 5 years in confinement by the juvenile court judge. Confinement will be in a juvenile detention facility. You can learn more about designated felony acts in Chapter Six of this book.

## IMPORTANT NOTES ABOUT PUNISHMENTS LISTED IN THIS BOOK:

**Adults only:** The punishments apply to persons prosecuted as adults for crimes (all persons 17 years old or older and persons over 13 years old who commit one of the seven deadly sins). Juvenile court judges will determine the punishment for persons who are prosecuted as juveniles in juvenile court.

**Imprisonment only:** The punishments address possible imprisonment, not possible fines.

**First time offenses:** The punishments apply the first time a person commits a crime. Repeated offenses of a crime will usually result in more severe punishments.

**Probation option:** Unless this book notes punishment in prison as having a "minimum" or "mandatory" sentence, the judge has the option of granting probation.

# CHAPTER TWO
## YOUR RIGHTS AS A TEENAGER:
## SEARCH AND SEIZURE

### Did You Know?

**DID YOU KNOW that if a police officer asks permission to search you, your pockets, your car, your book bag, or anything else that belongs to you, you always have the right to refuse to consent to the search?**

*Several high school students, all under 17 years old, skipped school during their lunch period and hung out in front of a McDonald's restaurant. A police officer approached the students and asked them their names. The officer then asked one of the students if the officer could see the contents of the student's pockets, and the student emptied his pockets. The student had a pill in his pocket that turned out to be Ritalin®. A friend had given him the pill earlier that day. The student was immediately arrested for possession of a Schedule II drug without a prescription.*

*When the student's attorney later asked him, "Why did you empty your pockets?," the student replied that he thought he was always supposed to do what a police officer asked. In this case, the officer did not have probable cause to search the student's pockets, but the evidence from the search was admissible in court because the student allowed the officer to see the contents of his pockets.*

Law students spend at least one entire semester of law school trying to learn the law on search and seizure of people and property and the laws involving an arrest. In the next two chapters, I explain some of the basic principles to give you an understanding of your rights. If you have any questions regarding your rights in a personal situation, you should consult with a lawyer.

The Fourth Amendment to the United States Constitution protects you against "unreasonable searches and seizures." The Fifth Amendment to the United States Constitution protects you against self-incrimination. The Sixth Amendment to the United States Constitution grants the right to a jury trial. The United States Supreme Court, the highest court in this country, has interpreted these Amendments in many cases. Interpretations of law by the Supreme Court are applicable to everyone in the United States. The discussion in Chapter Two and Chapter Three is based in part on interpretations of the Fourth, Fifth, and Sixth Amendments by the United States Supreme Court.

## REQUIREMENT OF PROBABLE CAUSE

All persons (including teenagers) are protected by the Fourth Amendment to the United States Constitution against unreasonable searches and seizures. In almost all cases, a police officer must have probable cause to search a person or property (including a vehicle). Probable cause exists when a reasonable person would believe that a crime was committed or that evidence of a crime is at a particular location. Probable cause requires more than suspicion. A police officer does not always have to get a search warrant before conducting a search. However, the police officer must have probable cause for the search, with certain limited exceptions. One of these exceptions is if you consent to the search.

## CONSENT TO SEARCHES

If a police officer has probable cause, the officer is not required to ask your permission to search you, your vehicle, or your belongings.

However, many times a police officer will ask you for consent (or permission) to search you, your vehicle, or your belongings. The officer makes this request because if you give consent, the officer is not required to have probable cause to conduct the search - you just gave the officer permission to do so. *If a police officer asks you for permission to search, you have the right to refuse to consent.* Many teenagers do not realize they have this right and tend to consent to whatever a police officer requests.

If a police officer asks you to consent to a search of you or your belongings, and you give consent, a judge will usually find the search to be valid even if the officer cannot show probable cause. Your consent will generally be enough to make a search lawful, even if the search may otherwise be unlawful. However, if you do not consent to a search, and the police officer cannot show probable cause to a judge, the judge can find that the search is not valid.

## 📣 *Pay Attention!*

**If an officer asks for your consent to search you, your vehicle, or your belongings, you should not voluntarily consent to the search. You should state clearly and respectfully that you do not consent. If the officer proceeds with a search, you should continue to be respectful, and you should not interfere with the search (or you may be guilty of obstruction of justice). Be sure to tell your attorney later that you did not consent to the search.**

### EXAMPLE:

*Person A is standing on a street corner in the middle of the afternoon. A police officer asks if the officer can look inside Person A's book bag. Person A should respectfully decline to consent to a search of Person A's book bag. Person A could respond, "No, I don't consent to a search of my book bag." Person A could also say, "I would like to call my parents (or another trusted adult)." If the police officer insists on continuing with a search, Person A should be respectful and cooperative. Later, if Person A is arrested, Person A should tell Person A's attorney that Person A did not consent to the search.*

### Other rules on consent:

- A child does not have the right to consent to a search of a parent's home.
- A parent has the right to give police consent to search a child's room in the parent's home or a child's car if owned by the parent. Even if you think it is your room because you do not share it with anyone, if it is in your parent's or guardian's house, your parent or guardian can give permission for the police to search the room without your consent to the search.
- A driver has the right to give an officer consent to search a vehicle. This rule applies even if the car is registered in someone else's name.

## SEARCHES OF PEOPLE

If a police officer has a <u>reasonable suspicion</u> that criminal activity has just taken place or is about to take place, the police officer may stop you and ask you questions. Reasonable suspicion is based on more than a hunch but less than probable cause. If and only if the police officer has reason to believe that you are armed and dangerous, the police officer can conduct a frisk. A frisk is a pat-down of your outer clothing. If and only if the officer develops probable cause during the frisk that evidence of a crime (such as drugs or weapons) is present, the officer has the right to search you.

> **EXAMPLE**
>
> *Someone reports seeing a teenager near school grounds with what appears to be a handgun and gives a description of the teenager to the police. A police officer arrives and sees a teenager who resembles the description. The police officer can stop the teenager and pat down the teenager's outer clothing for the officer's own safety. If the officer feels something that resembles a handgun inside the teenager's clothing, the officer can conduct a full search.*

After a police officer arrests a person for a crime, the officer has the right to search the person. The police officer does not need probable cause to search a person who is under arrest.

> **EXAMPLE**
>
> *The police arrest Person A for shoplifting. The police search Person A's pockets and find marijuana. The police do not need probable cause to search Person A's pockets because Person A is under arrest.*

A school board has the right to require drug testing of every student who participates in an extracurricular activity, such as sports or clubs. Drug testing of students is not considered a search under the law. Rather, drug testing is considered a condition of being allowed to participate in an activity. Think of it as flying on an airplane. As a condition of allowing you to fly, the airport has the right to search you and your luggage.

## SEARCHES OF VEHICLES

### ♀ *Did You Know?*

***DID YOU KNOW** that if the police stop you for a traffic violation, they can search your vehicle if they see or smell evidence of drugs or alcohol?*

*A state trooper stopped a 17 year old high school student for speeding. When the state trooper approached the vehicle, the state trooper smelled marijuana in the car. The state trooper ordered the driver and the passenger to exit the vehicle and then conducted a search of the vehicle for drugs. The state trooper found marijuana in the glove box between the driver and the passenger and arrested both for possession of marijuana.*

Police must have a reason before they can stop a vehicle. For example, if the officer sees a traffic offense (such as a tail light is out, or the tag is outdated, or the driver rolls through a stop sign), the officer has a reason to stop the vehicle. Police may also stop a vehicle if they have a reasonable suspicion that the vehicle was involved in criminal activity. In addition, police may establish a valid road block to check every driver that passes through the check point.

After the officer stops a vehicle for a valid reason, the officer may order the driver out of the vehicle even if the officer does not have reason to believe that the driver is involved in criminal activity. The officer may also order passengers out of the vehicle.

Police may, in certain circumstances, search vehicles without a search warrant:

- Police may search a vehicle if, after making a valid stop, the officer has probable cause to believe that evidence of a crime (such as drugs or weapons) is present.

> **EXAMPLE**
> *Person A, who is 16 years old, is driving a car with a tail light that is out. An officer stops Person A's car and sees beer in the car. Beer in the possession of a person under 21 years old is a crime, **even if the person has not been drinking.** The officer may search Person A's car without a warrant.*

- Police may search a vehicle if the officer arrests a driver or passenger and has probable cause to believe that evidence of the crime is in the car.

> **EXAMPLE**
> *Person A is driving a car erratically. The police stop Person A's car and arrest Person A for driving under the influence. The police may search Person A's car for drugs or alcohol without a warrant.*

- Police may search a vehicle if the officer impounds a vehicle after arresting the driver.

**✗ Exception:** If a passenger is capable of driving the vehicle, the police do not have a valid reason to impound the vehicle and conduct a search.

### EXAMPLE

*Person A is arrested for reckless driving and taken into custody. There are no passengers in the car. The police may impound Person A's car and search it later at the impound lot without a warrant. However, if Person B is a passenger in Person A's car and is capable of driving, Person A has the right to have Person B drive the car.*

## SEARCHES AT SCHOOLS

A school official may search a student, a student's locker, a student's book bag, or a student's car on school premises if the school official has reasonable suspicion that evidence of a crime (such as drugs or weapons) is present. Reasonable suspicion is based on more than a hunch but less than probable cause. Students must cooperate with a search by a school official.

However, a police officer must have *probable cause* to search a student, a student's locker, a student's book bag, or a student's car on school premises. If the police officer asks for the student's consent, the student has the right to refuse consent.

Some school systems employ "school resource officers" who are police officers. If the police officer is an employee of the school system, the officer has the same right to search as any school official. If you want to find out whether the school system or the police department employs a school resource officer, you may be able to tell from the school resource officer's uniform, or you can ask a school official.

Police officers may use drug sniffing dogs to sniff lockers, book bags, and cars on school premises if invited by school personnel. If a dog "hits" on a locker, book bag, or car, the police will have probable cause to search the contents.

# CHAPTER THREE
## *YOUR RIGHTS AS A TEENAGER: ARRESTS*

### DEFINITION OF ARREST AND POLICE QUESTIONING

### ♀ *Did You Know?*

*DID YOU KNOW that you do not have to be in handcuffs and the police officer does not have to say, "You are under arrest!" for you actually to be under arrest?*

*And...DID YOU KNOW that if you are stopped by police for questioning, you do not have to provide any information other than your name and birth date?*

Fortunately, most people who read this book will never be arrested. However, if you are arrested, you should know your rights under our laws. An arrest is the taking of a person into custody against the person's will for the purpose of criminal prosecution or interrogation. A police officer can only arrest you if the officer has probable cause to believe that you have committed a crime.

An arrest does not occur if a police officer simply approaches you and asks you questions. If a police officer has a reasonable suspicion that you may be involved in criminal activity, the officer may stop you and ask for identification. Reasonable suspicion is based on more than a hunch but less than probable cause. After you provide your name and birth date to the officer, you are not obligated to answer any more questions.  If you decide to answer questions beyond your name and birth date, the answers must be truthful. Giving false statements to law enforcement officials is a crime.

If the officer continues questioning, and you are not free to leave, the stop may be considered an arrest. A police officer does not have to say, "You are under arrest!" to place you under arrest. You do not have to be placed in handcuffs to be under arrest. The question is, after a brief questioning, were you free to leave? If a reasonable person would have felt free to leave, the officer has not made an arrest.

An officer does not need an arrest warrant if the officer has probable cause to arrest you, or if you commit a crime in the officer's presence.

If you are arrested, the police officer must tell you about your Miranda warnings before asking you more questions. You can learn more about Miranda warnings in the next section of this book.

### EXAMPLE

*A store manager sees Person A in the store for a long period of time.  Person A is carrying several bags, even though Person A has not made any purchases.  The store manager suspects that Person A has shoplifted some items and calls the police.  The police officer arrives and sees Person A coming out of the store holding several bags.  The officer has reasonable suspicion that Person A may be involved in criminal activity. The officer may stop Person A and inquire about Person A's name and birth date. However, if the officer asks questions about other things, such as the contents of the bags, Person A does not have to answer.*

*If the officer keeps Person A for more than a brief period of time and requires Person A to stay in an office at the store for further questioning, and Person A does not feel free to leave, Person A is technically under "arrest," even if the officer does not say that Person A is under arrest. The officer cannot continue questioning Person A without reading the Miranda warnings to Person A. Person A should not answer any questions (beyond providing name and birth date) and should ask to call an adult.*

## MIRANDA WARNINGS

Every person who has ever seen a cop show on television has heard the term "Miranda Warnings." These warnings are required because of a famous decision by the United States Supreme Court, *Miranda v. Arizona*. Miranda warnings are cautionary instructions that law enforcement officials must give a person in custody before interrogation. You are in custody if a) a police officer places you under arrest, or b) a police officer questions you in a situation in which a reasonable person does not feel free to leave. If you are in custody, the police must advise you of the following Miranda warnings:

- You have the right to remain silent.
- Anything you say can be used against you in a court of law.

- You have the right to have an attorney present during questioning.
- If you cannot afford an attorney, one will be appointed for you prior to questioning.
- You can terminate the questioning at any time and exercise any of these rights.

The police are not required to find you an attorney before they question you. **However, if you are under arrest and you ask for an attorney, the police cannot ask you any more questions until your attorney is present**. An attorney, a parent, or a guardian should be present before you answer any questions. If you are arrested, the fact that you ask to have an attorney present before answering any questions cannot be used against you later by a judge or a jury.

## ◀⑴ *Pay Attention!*
*If you are in police custody, request an attorney to be present before answering any questions.*

## POLICE QUESTIONING OF A PERSON UNDER 17 YEARS OLD WHO IS UNDER ARREST

A person under 17 years old who is under arrest may be questioned by the police just like any other suspect. The police will try to contact the parents or guardian before questioning and give them the opportunity to be present.

However, if the parents or guardian refuse to be present or cannot be located, the police can still question the suspect.

If you are under 17 years old and the police question you while under arrest, a judge will decide whether your statements can be used against you in court.  A judge will consider the following factors in determining whether your statements can be used against you:

- Your age
- Your education
- Your understanding of the charges being filed against you
- Your understanding of the Miranda warnings
- Whether you were allowed to communicate with parents, relatives, or a lawyer before being questioned
- Whether you were questioned before or after formal charges were filed against you
- The length of time police questioned you
- Whether you had refused to give statements on a prior occasion
- Whether you denied the contents of your statements at a later time

### ◀))  *Pay Attention!*
*If you are in police custody, request an attorney to be present before answering any questions.*

## FINGERPRINTING AND PHOTOGRAPHING A PERSON UNDER 17 YEARS OLD WHO IS CHARGED WITH A CRIME

If you are under 17 years old, and the police charge you with a felony crime, the police will take you into custody and fingerprint and photograph you.

The juvenile court judge may release your name, address, and the crimes charged against you to the local school superintendent and/or to the Department of Family and Children Services. The school superintendent may share this information with your teachers and counselors.

If the charges against you are later dismissed, you can apply to have fingerprint information and photographs destroyed.

# CHAPTER FOUR
## PARTIES TO A CRIME
## (WHO CAN BE CHARGED WITH A CRIME)

### ⚲ Did You Know?
**DID YOU KNOW that you can be guilty of a crime even if you only have a small part in planning it?**

In some cases, young people have told me that they should not be charged with a crime because they did not actually "participate" in the crime. However, all persons involved in committing, planning, participating, helping, advising, encouraging, or benefiting in the criminal activity are parties to the crime. If you had anything to do with committing the crime, no matter how minor the involvement may be, you can be convicted of the crime.

> **EXAMPLE**
> *Persons A, B, C, and D, who are 17 years old, plan an armed robbery of a convenience store. Person A drives the car, Person B stands look-out at the door, Person C holds the gun and demands the money from the cashier, and Person D stays home and waits for Persons A, B, and C to return with the money. Persons A, B, C, and D are all guilty of armed robbery. If convicted, each will have to serve a minimum of 10 years in prison without parole.*

**EXAMPLE**

*In the previous example, Person A accidentally hits a pedestrian with the car when leaving the convenience store, and the pedestrian dies. Persons A, B, C, and D are all guilty of felony murder, even though Person A was driving and none of the people involved planned on hurting anyone in the robbery. If convicted, Persons A, B, C, and D will be punished with life in prison with the possibility of parole after 25 years, life in prison without parole, or death. (You can read more about felony murder in Chapter Twenty-One of this book.)*

## 📢 Pay Attention!

**When your friends do a crime, you may also do the time. Beware the company you keep!**

# CHAPTER FIVE
## PROSECUTION AS AN ADULT

## HAPPY 17th BIRTHDAY!

### ♀ Did You Know?
**DID YOU KNOW that when you turn 17 years old, you are an adult under Georgia's criminal laws?**

You wake up on your 17th birthday and you might wonder, "What is different about today from yesterday?" There is a big difference! From this point forward, you must be prosecuted and punished as any other adult if you commit a crime in Georgia. (In some states, the age is 18.) On your 17th birthday, while you are restricted from voting, drinking alcohol, and buying cigarettes, you are an adult under criminal laws.

Any arrest that you receive after reaching your 17th birthday may remain on your criminal history record for the remainder of your life. You will probably have to provide a copy of your criminal history record when you apply for a job or apply to attend college or technical school. If you are able to have your case dismissed, you may be able to get the arrest expunged (erased) from your criminal history record.

**EXAMPLE**

*Person A is 17 years old and is convicted of shoplifting along with Person B who is 16 years old. Person A must be prosecuted and punished as an adult. Person B will be prosecuted in juvenile court and sentenced as a juvenile offender.*

In Georgia, if a person 17 years old or older commits murder with "aggravating circumstances" and is convicted, the person could be sentenced to death.

## SEVEN DEADLY SINS: PROSECUTION AS AN ADULT FOR PERSONS 13, 14, 15, AND 16 YEARS OLD

## ⚲ Did You Know?

**DID YOU KNOW that persons 13-16 years old can be prosecuted as adults for the seven deadly sins?**

*A 15 year old, 16 year old, and 17 year old were all charged with armed robbery of a convenience store with a firearm. The 15 year old and 16 year old were prosecuted as adults along with the 17 year old. They each were sentenced to the mandatory 10 years in prison without parole.*

A person 13, 14, 15 or 16 years old may be prosecuted and punished as an adult if the person is charged with any of the following crimes, which are known as the "seven deadly sins":
• Murder (including felony murder)

- Voluntary manslaughter
- Rape
- Aggravated sodomy
- Aggravated child molestation
- Aggravated sexual battery
- Armed robbery if committed with a firearm

**EXAMPLE**

*Person A is 13 years old and is arrested for rape. Person A can be prosecuted as if Person A were an adult and, if convicted, must serve a minimum sentence of 25 years in prison without parole and can be sentenced to a maximum of life in prison.*

The district attorney, and only the district attorney, makes the decision whether a person under 17 years old will be prosecuted as an adult. The district attorney may, in some extraordinary circumstances, send a case to juvenile court.

Once the prosecution begins, a superior court judge may send the case back to juvenile court if a) the person is charged with voluntary manslaughter, aggravated child molestation, or aggravated sexual battery, and b) the superior court judge finds that there is an extraordinary reason to send the case to juvenile court.

If a person commits a murder when the person is under 17 years old, the prosecutor cannot seek the death penalty as punishment.

A juvenile court judge may refer some cases involving persons 13-16 years old to superior court. You can learn more about referrals by juvenile court judges in Chapter Six of this book.

# CHAPTER SIX
## PROSECUTION OF PERSONS
## UNDER 17 YEARS OLD

### ♀ Did You Know?

**DID YOU KNOW that the juvenile court judge usually decides your criminal case if you are under 17 years old?**

*Three 16 year olds were caught by the police throwing toilet paper in the trees in the front yard of a home owned by a school teacher. They were each charged with criminal trespass, and their case was sent to juvenile court where a juvenile court judge decided their guilt and punishment.*

## JUVENILE COURT

Juvenile courts have jurisdiction and control of most legal issues involving persons under 17 years old.

If you are under 17 years old and find yourself in juvenile court, a judge, rather than a jury, will decide your guilt or innocence. Before a judge decides on a guilty verdict (which is called an "adjudication of delinquency"), you will have the choice to plead guilty or to plead innocent to the offense. If you plead innocent, the prosecution must prove to the judge that you are guilty beyond reasonable doubt.

If the judge finds you guilty of an offense in juvenile court, the judge has a wide range of possible sentences, including incarceration, fines, community service, drug/alcohol courses, suspension of driver's license or learner's permit, and mandatory education.

Juvenile court records are confidential and, in most cases, are not available to the public. Offenses prosecuted in juvenile court are called delinquent acts, rather than crimes.

If a juvenile court rules that you have committed a delinquent act, you can honestly state on future college or job applications that you have not been convicted of a crime.

Under certain circumstances, related to the number and type of offenses that a person has committed, a juvenile court judge may transfer persons 13-16 years old to superior court to be prosecuted – as an adult – by the district attorney's office.

**EXAMPLE**
*A juvenile court judges finds Person A, a 15 year old, guilty of shoplifting. Person A has never been prosecuted as an adult in superior or state court. If applying for a job, Person A can honestly state, "I have never been convicted of a crime," because Person A has only been found guilty of a delinquent act in juvenile court (and not found guilty of a crime as an adult in superior or state court).*

Juvenile courts also handle cases involving unruly children (such as a truant), deprived children (children who are without food, shelter or protection), and girls under 18 years old who want an abortion without the knowledge of their parents.

## DELINQUENT ACT/ DELINQUENT CHILD

A delinquent act is an act committed by a person under 17 years old that would be a crime if the act were committed by a person 17 years old or older. A delinquent act is not technically considered a crime unless the act is one of the seven deadly sins for which a person 13 years old or older can be prosecuted as an adult, such as armed robbery with a firearm. You can learn more about the seven deadly sins in Chapter Five of this book.

A delinquent child is a person under 17 years old who has committed a delinquent act and is in need of treatment or rehabilitation.

> **EXAMPLE**
> *Person A is 16 years old and is convicted of shoplifting video games worth under $300. Person A will be prosecuted in juvenile court for a delinquent act. If Person A is 17 years old and is convicted of shoplifting video games worth under $300, Person A will be prosecuted as an adult for a misdemeanor.*

**EXAMPLE**

*Person A is 15 years old. Person A approaches Person B with a gun and demands Person B's MP3 player. Person B gives the MP3 player to Person A. Person A is guilty of armed robbery, one of the seven deadly sins, and may be prosecuted as an adult in superior court for a felony.*

# DESIGNATED FELONY ACT FOR JUVENILE OFFENDERS

## ♀ Did You Know?

**DID YOU KNOW that for some offenses in juvenile court, a judge can send you to jail when you are under 17 years old?**

You can go to jail if you commit a criminal act when you are under 17 years old, particularly if the crime is a designated felony act. A designated felony act for juvenile offenders 13, 14, 15 or 16 years old is a criminal act with a sentence of up to 5 years in confinement. The juvenile court judge determines the length of confinement. Confinement for a designated felony act will be in a juvenile detention facility.

The following are some of the crimes that are designated felony acts:

- Aggravated assault
- Aggravated battery
- Robbery
- Armed robbery (without a firearm)
- Battery on a school teacher or other school personnel
- Kidnapping
- Arson
- Attempted murder
- Attempted kidnapping
- Hijacking a motor vehicle
- Second conviction for possession of a pistol
- Trafficking in cocaine, marijuana, methamphetamine, or other illegal drugs
- Participation in criminal street gang activity
- Possession of a weapon in a school safety zone

# CHAPTER SEVEN
## *TRIAL AND PUNISHMENT*

Most people gain their entire knowledge about criminal trials from television. If you have never seen a real criminal trial, I encourage you to visit your local courthouse. When I worked in the district attorney's office, student groups often visited and watched all or a portion of a trial. If time permits, you may be able to ask the prosecutor and defense attorney questions during breaks.

## SUGGESTIONS IF YOU ARE SUMMONED TO COURT

The following are some suggestions if you are summoned to appear in court because you received a traffic violation or a county ordinance violation or because you are arrested for a crime or delinquent act:

- Consult with an attorney about your situation. A brief consultation with an attorney may be free of charge. You may or may not actually have to hire an attorney, depending on the seriousness of your case.

- Always appear in court on your court date if you are required to go to court. Even if you do not have an attorney, you must answer the summons to appear in court by showing up. If you fail to appear in court on

your court date, you may be arrested for contempt of court, and your punishment may be increased. Don't complicate your situation!
- Be on time when you go to court!
- If you are charged with a crime where the possible punishment is more than 6 months in prison, and you cannot afford an attorney, the judge will appoint an attorney to represent you.
- Dress appropriately. My suggestion is to dress as if you are going to a religious service or a funeral. When you dress nicely, you are showing respect to the judge.
- Do not take cell phones or pagers into a courtroom.
- Do not wear a cap or a hat in the courtroom.
- Do not chew gum or take food or drink into a courtroom.
- Always be respectful and look the judge in the eye. Answer with "Yes, Your Honor" or "No, Your Honor" when being questioned by the judge.

## PROOF OF GUILT AND JURY TRIALS

The prosecutor must be able to prove that a person accused of a crime is guilty beyond a reasonable doubt. A person may also admit guilt and plead guilty to a crime.

If you are 17 years old or older and are charged with a misdemeanor or a felony, you have the right under the Sixth

Amendment to the United States Constitution to have your guilt decided by a jury. If you are under 17 years old and are prosecuted as an adult in superior court, you also have the right to a jury trial. A person may waive the right to a jury trial and have guilt or innocence determined by a judge.

If you are under 17 years old and are prosecuted in juvenile court, you do not have the right to a jury trial. A judge will determine your guilt or innocence.

In Georgia, in all cases except death penalty cases, the judge (rather than the jury) decides the punishment for a crime.

## IMPRISONMENT

If you are sentenced to spend time in prison, factors such as your age, the type of crime, and the judge's sentence determine where you will serve the sentence.

If you are under 17 years old and are sentenced to confinement, you will be sent to a state youth detention center. However, if you are convicted of one of the seven deadly sins, and the confinement extends beyond your 17th birthday, you will be transferred to an adult facility when you turn 17.

If you are 17 years old or older and are sentenced to less than a year in jail, you will serve the time in the county jail. If you are 17 years old or older and are sentenced to more than a year in prison, you will serve the time in one of Georgia's state prisons.

A person in prison may possibly be eligible for release before the end of a prison sentence if the Department of Pardons and Parole grants an early release (or parole). However, some serious crimes have punishments with minimum or mandatory sentences or prison time without the possibility of parole, and persons who commit these crimes are not eligible for parole.

## PROBATION

Probation is punishment served outside of prison, but there's a catch. Probation is usually conditioned on certain restrictions or requirements, including:

- Payment of a probation supervision fee to a probation officer
- Payment of a fine
- Payment of restitution (damages), if any, to the victim
- No use of alcohol or drugs
- Random drug and alcohol tests
- Community service
- Avoidance of people of bad character (such as other

people who may be on probation)
- Waiver of rights protected by the Fourth Amendment to the United States Constitution

The last condition above means that a probation officer or law enforcement officer can search you, your home, or your car without a search warrant or probable cause while you are on probation.

If a judge decides that you have violated a condition of probation, the judge can sentence you to spend the rest or a portion of the remaining sentence in prison.

> **EXAMPLE**
> *Person A, who is 17 years old, is convicted of driving under the influence, a misdemeanor. The judge sentences Person A to ten days in jail followed by probation of 11 months and 20 days. On the 10th day of probation, Person A fails a drug/alcohol screening. The judge can sentence Person A to the remaining time, 11 months and 10 days, in the county jail.*

For most crimes, a judge has the discretion to grant probation for all or a portion of a sentence. For example, a person may receive straight probation without any prison time, or a person may serve a portion of a sentence in prison and a portion of a sentence on probation.

For serious crimes with mandatory or minimum prison time, judges cannot grant probation in lieu of these punishments.

## FINES

Judges may impose fines for felonies and misdemeanors in addition to other punishment. Fines for most misdemeanors do not exceed $1000. Fines for most felonies exceed $1000 and may be $100,000 or greater depending on the crime.

# PART II: WHAT'S THE CRIME?

DRUGS AND ALCOHOL

VEHICLES

SEX CRIMES

HARM TO PEOPLE

HARM TO PROPERTY

MORE CRIMES

# CHAPTER EIGHT
## *UNDERAGE DRINKING*

The legal age to purchase and consume alcohol in this country is 21. (You can consume alcohol if you are under 21 under very limited circumstances as discussed below.)

One of the most frequent ways that persons under 21 years old get in trouble with the law in Georgia is due to possession and/or consumption of alcohol. But not only teenagers get in trouble; sometimes parents get in trouble when they allow teenagers who are not their own children to consume alcohol in their home. This chapter describes common alcohol-related crimes that affect persons under 21 years old other than driving under the influence of alcohol or drugs (DUI), which is discussed in Chapter Thirteen.

## PURCHASE OR POSSESSION OF ALCOHOL BY PERSONS UNDER 21 YEARS OLD (M.I.P.-MINOR IN POSSESSION)

### 𝒫 *Did You Know?*
*DID YOU KNOW that alcohol on the breath is enough evidence to charge a person under 21 with possession of alcohol?*

ⓘ **A crime occurs when a person under 21 years old purchases, attempts to purchase, or possesses alcoholic beverages.**

Possession of alcohol does not mean you have to have a container of alcohol with you; alcohol on your breath is sufficient.

## ✕ Exceptions:
- If you possess alcohol for medical reasons and have a valid prescription given by a licensed doctor
- If you possess alcohol as part of a religious ceremony
- If your parent or guardian gives the alcoholic beverage to you while your parent or guardian is present and you are in your parent's or guardian's home
- If you serve or sell alcohol as part of your lawful employment

*Type of crime:* Misdemeanor
*Punishment:* Up to 6 months imprisonment *and* 120-day suspension of learner's permit or driver's license for a person under 21 years old

> **EXAMPLE**
> *Person A is under 21 years old, and Person A's parents serve Person A a glass of wine in their home at dinner. Neither Person A nor Person A's parents are in violation of the law.*

**EXAMPLE**

*Person A is under 21 years old and attends a party at Person B's house. Person B's parent provides beer, which Person A drinks. Person A is guilty of unlawful possession and/or consumption of alcohol.*

**EXAMPLE**

*Person A is under 21 years old and is a member of the Catholic faith. Person A is served wine during a religious service in church. Person A is not violating the law.*

## ♀ Did You Know?

**DID YOU KNOW that you may be arrested if you are under 21 years old and attend a party where other people are drinking, even if you have not been drinking?**

If alcohol is present and available for everyone at a party, the officer has probable cause to believe that any person present is drinking alcohol and may arrest everyone under 21 years old. Of course, being arrested is not the same as being convicted of a crime. You would still have a defense that you were not drinking.

## ◀🔊 Pay Attention!

**If you are at a party with alcohol, and the police arrest you, you should request that the officer give you a breathalyzer test immediately if you have not been drinking.**

## FURNISHING ALCOHOL TO PERSONS UNDER 21 YEARS OLD

*A parent of a high school student provided her child and several of her child's friends, all of whom were under 21 years old, with beer during a spend the night party in her home. The parent did not allow anyone to drive and required everyone to stay at the house. However, neighbors called the police to complain of loud noise at the party. Police arrived at the party and discovered that persons under 21 had consumed alcohol given to them by the parent. The parent was charged with unlawful furnishing of alcohol to minors.*

(i) *A crime occurs when a person provides alcoholic beverages to a person under 21 years old.*

## ✗ Exceptions:

- If the person under 21 years old requires alcohol for medical reasons and has a valid prescription given by a licensed doctor
- If the person under 21 years old possesses alcohol as part of a religious ceremony
- If the parent or guardian of a child under 21 years old gives the alcoholic beverage to the child while the parent or guardian is present and in the parent's or guardian's home
- If an employer employs a person under 21 years old who serves or sells alcohol as part of the person's lawful employment

**EXAMPLE**

*A college social organization decides to have a keg party and serve beer. A 21 year old goes to the liquor store and purchases the keg. If any person under 21 years old attends the party and consumes the beer, the 21 year old can be charged with providing alcohol to a minor, with a separate charge for each minor.*

## Did You Know?

**DID YOU KNOW that if you are under 21 years old and provide alcohol to someone under 21 years old, you can still be charged with the crime of unlawful furnishing of alcohol to a minor?**

*Type of crime:* Misdemeanor
*Punishment:* Up to 12 months imprisonment

## CIVIL LIABILITY FOR FURNISHING ALCOHOL TO AN UNDERAGE PERSON

In addition to criminal liability, an adult may also face civil liability for providing alcohol to a person under 21 years old. With civil liability, an adult may be required to pay significant damages for any injury or damage that may result from the minor's drinking.

(i) **An adult may have civil liability for providing alcohol to an underage person if the adult willfully, knowingly, and unlawfully 1) serves alcohol to a minor or furnishes or sells alcohol to a minor and 2) knows (or should know) that the minor will soon be driving a motor vehicle.**

> **EXAMPLE**
>
> *Person A throws a party at Person A's house. Alcohol is present at the party. Person A's parents know that Person B is under 21 years old and that Person B consumes alcohol while at the party. Person A's parents also know that Person B's car is parked out front. Person B leaves the party and is involved in an accident that seriously injures a passenger in Person B's car as well as the other driver. If the accident occurred because Person B was a less safe driver due to the alcohol, Person A's parents could be liable for the injuries.*

## EMPLOYMENT INVOLVING ALCOHOLIC BEVERAGES

If you are under 18 years old, you may not dispense, serve, sell, or take orders for alcoholic beverages unless you are employed in a supermarket, convenience store, brewery, or drug store where the alcohol will be consumed off the premises.

If you are 18, 19, or 20 years old, you may dispense, serve, sell, handle, take orders for, or possess alcohol as part of your employment in a licensed establishment (such as a restaurant).

# CHAPTER NINE
## FALSE IDENTIFICATION AND MISREPRESENTATION OF AGE

### ♀ Did You Know?

**DID YOU KNOW that possessing a false identification document with a government logo is a felony in Georgia?**

*A 20 year old college student and her best friend went to a bar near campus to drink beer. A police officer asked to see their identifications, and the girls showed the officer fake drivers' licenses with a government logo of the State of Florida. Both girls were arrested for underage purchase of alcohol, a misdemeanor, but they were also arrested for possessing a false identification with a governmental logo, a felony! Because they were arrested on a felony charge, it took almost two days before they could get out of jail on bond.*

Possessing a false identification with a government logo was made a felony after the 9/11 terrorist attacks in 2001. In 2007, the state legislature tried to reduce it to a misdemeanor, but the bill was vetoed, so it is still a felony today.

## POSSESSION OF FALSE IDENTIFICATION OR ANOTHER PERSON'S ID TO PURCHASE ALCOHOL

A false identification document contains inaccurate information about your identity and appears to be issued by a government agency or other official authority but was not actually issued by the government agency or other official authority.

Sometimes teenagers use their own false identification document to misrepresent their age, and sometimes they use another person's identification document (either false or valid) to misrepresent their age in order to purchase alcohol or be admitted to a bar.

ⓘ *A crime occurs when a person under 21 years old misrepresents the person's identity or uses any false identification for the purpose of purchasing an alcoholic beverage.*

*Type of crime:* Misdemeanor
*Punishment:* Up to 12 months imprisonment *and* 6-month suspension of learner's permit or driver's license for a person under 21 years old.

## 🔊 *Pay Attention!*

*Important Exception: If you possess or use a false identification document for any reason which appears to contain a logo or legal or official seal of a government agency, then the crime is a felony, and the punishment is 1 to 5 years imprisonment.*

## MAKING, SELLING, OR DISTRIBUTING FALSE IDENTIFICATION

**(i) *A crime occurs when a person makes, sells, distributes, delivers, or possesses with intent to sell false identification documents.***

*Type of crime:* Misdemeanor
*Punishment:* Up to 12 months imprisonment

## 📢 *Pay Attention!*

*Important Exception: If you make, sell, distribute, deliver, or possess with intent to sell a false identification document which appears to have the logo or legal or official seal of a government agency, then the crime is a felony, and the punishment is 1 to 5 years imprisonment.*

*AND PAY ATTENTION AGAIN!! Another Important Exception: If you make, sell, distribute, deliver, receive, possess, or offer for sale 3 or more false identification documents – with or without the logo or legal or official seal of a government agency - the crime is a felony, and the punishment is 3 to 10 years imprisonment.*

**EXAMPLE**

*A college social organization has a machine that makes false identification documents. Person A makes 25 false identification documents, Person B delivers them to Person C, and Person C distributes them to 25 members of the social organization. Person A, Person B, and Person C may each be charged with a felony.*

# CHAPTER TEN
## *POSSESSION AND SALE OF MARIJUANA*

Next to underage drinking, possession and distribution of marijuana are some of the most common violations of law among young people. People often ask, "Why is possessing marijuana for your own personal use against the law?" That question has been debated for decades and is still being debated today across this country. Regardless of the debate, possessing, distributing, and selling marijuana are still against the law.

The following is a description of some of the laws and penalties relating to the possession and sale or distribution of marijuana.

## POSSESSION OF LESS THAN AN OUNCE OF MARIJUANA

*Type of crime:* Misdemeanor
*Punishment:* Up to 12 months imprisonment *and* 6-month suspension of learner's permit or driver's license

## POSSESSION OF MORE THAN AN OUNCE OF MARIJUANA

 *Type of crime:* Felony
*Punishment:* 1 to 10 years imprisonment *and* 6-month suspension of learner's permit or driver's license

## SALE, DELIVERY, DISTRIBUTION, OR POSSESSION WITH INTENT TO DISTRIBUTE ANY AMOUNT OF MARIJUANA

*Type of crime:* Felony
*Punishment:* 1 to 10 years imprisonment *and* 6-month suspension of learner's permit or driver's license

## ♀ *Did You Know?*

**DID YOU KNOW that sharing a joint with a friend - even for free - is distribution of marijuana and can get you 10 years in prison if you are 17 years old or older?**

**EXAMPLE**

*Person A is smoking a joint and shares it with Person B. Person A is guilty of distributing marijuana, a felony. Person B is guilty of misdemeanor possession of marijuana. If Person B passes the joint back to Person A, Person B is also guilty of distributing marijuana, a felony.*

The manner in which marijuana is packaged may determine whether the police believe marijuana is packaged for personal consumption or for distribution.

> **EXAMPLE**
>
> *Person A has one plastic bag with less than an ounce of marijuana. Person A will probably be charged with simple possession (misdemeanor).*
>
> **EXAMPLE**
>
> *Person B has 6 plastic bags containing a total of less than an ounce of marijuana. Person B will probably be charged with possession with intent to distribute marijuana (felony).*

# CHAPTER ELEVEN
## POSSESSION AND SALE OF OTHER ILLEGAL DRUGS OR LEGAL DRUGS WITHOUT A VALID PRESCRIPTION

### ℗ Did You Know?
**DID YOU KNOW that giving a prescription drug to a friend is a crime and that possessing a prescription drug that doesn't belong to you is a crime?**

*A 17 year old high school senior sat outside during lunch period at school visiting with her best friend who was not feeling well. The senior had a valid prescription for Tylenol III® in her purse and gave her friend one of her pills. A school police officer observed the exchange and arrested both girls. The senior was arrested for distribution of a Schedule III drug, and her friend was arrested for possession of a Schedule III drug without a prescription. Because Tylenol III® is a Schedule III drug, both the senior and her friend were charged with felonies.*

In most cases involving teenagers and illegal drugs, teenagers usually know that what they are doing is against the law. However, many teenagers do not know that giving a prescription drug, even just one pill, to a friend is a crime. Only pharmacists and health care providers can give another person a prescription drug.

## ◀))  Pay Attention!

**If someone asks you for one of your prescription pills, say NO. Otherwise, you could be charged with a crime. This is one time that it's OK to be selfish and not share!**

Georgia law classifies various drugs as Schedule I, II, III, IV, and V drugs depending on whether the drug has a legitimate purpose and whether the drug can be addictive and subject to abuse. Prescription drugs that are not on Schedules I-V are called "dangerous drugs." The following describes the classification of drugs in Georgia:

<u>Schedule I drugs</u> are those drugs that have no legitimate medical purpose, such as LSD, heroin, ecstasy (a/k/a E), and GHB (a/k/a Georgia Home Boy).

<u>Schedule II drugs</u> are those drugs that have a medical purpose but have a high potential for abuse, such as Ritalin®, OxyContin®, Adderall®, cocaine (a/k/a crack), opium, methamphetamine (a/k/a ice or crystal), and morphine.

<u>Schedule III, IV, and V drugs</u> are those drugs that have a medical purpose but have some potential for abuse, with Schedule V drugs having the lowest potential for abuse. Some common drugs are Vicodin® and Tylenol III® (Schedule III drugs) and Xanax®, Librium®, Ativan®, and Rohypnol® (a/k/a roofies) (Schedule IV drugs).

<u>Dangerous Drugs</u> are prescription drugs that are not included on Schedules I-V. Amoxicillin® and Viagra® are examples of dangerous drugs.

The following describes some of the laws and penalties relating to Schedule I, II, III, IV, and V drugs and dangerous drugs.

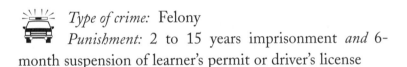

## POSSESSION OF ANY SCHEDULE I OR SCHEDULE II DRUG WITHOUT A VALID PRESCRIPTION

 *Type of crime:* Felony
*Punishment:* 2 to 15 years imprisonment *and* 6-month suspension of learner's permit or driver's license

## SALE, DELIVERY, DISTRIBUTION, OR POSSESSION WITH INTENT TO DISTRIBUTE ANY SCHEDULE I OR II DRUG

 *Type of crime:* Felony
*Punishment:* 5 to 30 years imprisonment *and* 6-month suspension of learner's permit or driver's license

## POSSESSION OF ANY SCHEDULE III, IV, OR V DRUG WITHOUT A VALID PRESCRIPTION

 *Type of crime:* Felony
*Punishment:* 1 to 5 years imprisonment *and* 6-month suspension of learner's permit or driver's license

### ◀))) *Pay Attention!*

**Punishment for possession of Rohypnol® (a/k/a roofies, a common date rape drug) is 2 to 15 years imprisonment**

## SALE, DELIVERY, DISTRIBUTION, OR POSSESSION WITH INTENT TO DISTRIBUTE ANY SCHEDULE III, IV, OR V DRUG

 *Type of crime:* Felony
*Punishment:* 1 to 10 years imprisonment *and* 6-month suspension of learner's permit or driver's license

### ◀))) *Pay Attention!*

**Punishment for giving Rohypnol® (a/k/a roofies, a common date rape drug) to another person is 5 to 30 years imprisonment**

# SALE, DISTRIBUTION, OR POSSESSION OF A DANGEROUS DRUG

 *Type of crime:* Misdemeanor
*Punishment:* Up to 12 months imprisonment

# CHAPTER TWELVE
## *OTHER DRUG-RELATED LAWS*

## ASKING A PERSON UNDER 17 YEARS OLD TO DELIVER ILLEGAL DRUGS

(i) *A crime occurs when a person hires, solicits, or uses another person under 17 years old to manufacture, distribute, or deliver marijuana or other illegal drugs (including counterfeit drugs).*

*Type of crime:* Felony
*Punishment:* 5 to 20 years imprisonment

### EXAMPLE

*Person A asks Person B, who is 15 years old, to deliver to Person C less than an ounce of marijuana. Person B delivers marijuana to Person C. Person A is guilty of a felony for asking Person B to deliver marijuana. Person B may be prosecuted in juvenile court for delivering marijuana. Person C, if caught with less than an ounce of marijuana, is guilty of a misdemeanor.*

## INHALATION OF MODEL GLUE

**A crime occurs when a person intentionally smells or inhales the fumes from model glue.**

 *Type of crime:* Misdemeanor
*Punishment:* Up to 12 months imprisonment

## POSSESSION OF DRUG RELATED OBJECT

**A crime occurs when a person uses, or has in the person's possession with the intent to use, an object for inhaling, storing, packaging, growing, or concealing marijuana, illegal drugs, or other dangerous drugs.**

> **EXAMPLE**
>
> *Person A has in Person A's possession a bong that is used for smoking marijuana. The police can show that the bong is typically used for the purpose of smoking marijuana. Even if no marijuana is actually present, Person A can be charged with a crime.*

*Type of crime:* Misdemeanor
*Punishment:* Up to 12 months imprisonment

## ILLEGAL DRUGS IN A SCHOOL SAFETY ZONE

### ♀ Did You Know?

**DID YOU KNOW that sharing a blunt with a friend on school property is a felony?**

*Two teenagers shared a blunt while sitting on a bench on a school playground. The school had been permanently closed, but the school system still owned the property. Both teenagers were arrested for distributing marijuana within 1000 feet of a school or property owned by a school system, a felony.*

**(i)** **A crime occurs when a person manufactures, distributes, dispenses, or possesses with intent to distribute any illegal drug or any amount of marijuana within 1000 feet of any public or private elementary school, middle school, high school, school bus, or property owned by a school board.**

The school does not have to be in session.

*Type of crime:* Felony
*Punishment:* Up to 20 years imprisonment

**EXAMPLE**

*Person A plays in the high school band and is on a school bus coming home from a football game. Person A is caught with several packages of marijuana in Person A's pockets. Person A may be charged with possession of marijuana with intent to distribute in a school safety zone.*

## ILLEGAL DRUGS NEAR A PARK OR PUBLIC HOUSING PROJECT

 **A crime occurs when a person manufactures, distributes, dispenses, or possesses with intent to distribute any illegal drug or any amount of marijuana within 1000 feet of a public park, playground, recreation center, or public housing project.**

*Type of crime:* Felony
*Punishment:* Up to 20 years imprisonment

## MANUFACTURE, DISTRIBUTION, OR POSSESSION OF FAKE ILLEGAL DRUGS

 **A crime occurs when a person knowingly manufactures, distributes, or possesses with the intent to**

**distribute anything that is alleged to be an illegal drug but is actually an imitation (such as a fake substance).**

*Type of crime:* Misdemeanor

*Punishment:* Up to 12 months imprisonment

**EXAMPLE**

*Person A sells Person B a substance and tells Person B that the substance is marijuana, when, in fact, it is harmless grass. Person A is guilty of a misdemeanor.*

## FIRST OFFENSE FOR POSSESSION OF ILLEGAL DRUGS

If you are charged with possession of marijuana or other illegal drugs for the first time, you may be able to avoid a conviction under certain circumstances.

You, the prosecutor, and the judge must agree to defer the sentencing with certain conditions, such as:
- You will be put on probation and cannot violate any law while on probation. The judge can require probation for up to 3 years.
- You may be required to undergo a drug rehabilitation program, including a drug and alcohol evaluation and medical treatment, if necessary.
- Your driver's license may be suspended for 6 months.

- If you successfully complete all the conditions of probation, the judge can dismiss the charges, and you will not
  have a conviction on your record.

### 📢 *Pay Attention!*
*You only have one chance to be a first offender.*

# CHAPTER THIRTEEN
## DRINKING, DRUGS, AND DRIVING

### ♀ Did You Know?

**DID YOU KNOW that a person under 21 years old can be charged with driving under the influence (DUI) if the person's alcohol concentration is .02 grams or higher?**

**And.....DID YOU KNOW that for most people under 21 years old, drinking only one beer or one glass of wine or one mixed drink will cause their alcohol concentration to be .02 grams or higher?**

**And.....DID YOU KNOW that you can be arrested for DUI if you are involved in an accident, even if the accident is not your fault?**

*A freshman in college attended a party with a date and drank one beer. As he was driving his date home, another driver ran a red light and T-boned the college student's car. Fortunately, no one was seriously injured in the accident. The police officer on the scene smelled alcohol on the college student's breath and gave him a breathalyzer test. His alcohol concentration registered .03 grams. Although the other driver was at fault and was given a ticket for running the red light, the student was arrested and taken to jail for DUI.*

Sometimes teenagers are in accidents where they are totally without fault for the cause of the accident. However, if the officer investigating the accident smells alcohol on the teenager's breath, the officer may arrest the teenager for DUI, even though the alcohol was not the cause of the accident.

## DRIVING UNDER THE INFLUENCE OF ALCOHOL OR DRUGS

(i) *The crime of driving under the influence of alcohol or drugs (DUI) occurs when a person drives a motorized vehicle (such as a car, truck, motorcycle, bus, motor boat, or jet ski) under any of the following conditions:*

- *Under the influence of alcohol to the extent it is less safe for the person to drive*
- *With an alcohol concentration of .02 grams or more within 3 hours of driving a vehicle if the driver is under 21 years old*
- *With an alcohol concentration of .08 grams or more within 3 hours of driving a vehicle if the driver is 21 years old or older*
- *Under the influence of any legal drug to the extent it is less safe for the person to drive*
- *Under the influence of marijuana to the extent it is less safe for the person to drive*
- *With any amount of an illegal drug, other than marijuana, in the blood or urine*

**EXAMPLE**

*Person A is 18 years old and consents to a breathalyzer or blood test. The test shows an alcohol concentration of .02. Person A is guilty of DUI.*

**EXAMPLE**

*Person A is driving with marijuana in Person A's blood or urine. The prosecution must prove that Person A was also a less safe driver (for example, committed excessive speeding, weaving, or reckless driving) for Person A to be guilty of DUI.*

**EXAMPLE**

*Person A is 17 years old and does not consent to a breathalyzer or blood test. The officer smells alcohol or sees an alcohol container. The prosecution must prove that Person A is a less safe driver (for example, committed excessive speeding, weaving, or reckless driving) because of the alcohol to be guilty of DUI.*

*Type of crime:* Misdemeanor
*Punishment:* Up to 12 months imprisonment *and* 6-month suspension of learner's permit or driver's license for a person under 21 years old (or 12-month suspension if alcohol concentration is .08 grams or more)

## Did You Know?

**DID YOU KNOW that for a first DUI, you must spend at least 24 hours in jail and that for a second DUI, you must spend at least 72 hours in jail?**

## ℘ Did You Know?

*And...DID YOU KNOW that if you are guilty of DUI, and there is a passenger under the age of 14 in the car, you are also guilty of a separate crime: endangering the life of a child? This crime is a misdemeanor.*

## IMPLIED CONSENT AND THE BREATHALYZER TEST

If a police officer has probable cause and arrests you for driving under the influence of alcohol or drugs (DUI), the officer is required to ask you whether you are willing to consent to a breathalyzer or blood alcohol test. If you have a learner's permit or driver's license, you have essentially given your <u>implied consent</u> to a breathalyzer or blood alcohol test in exchange for the privilege of driving. However, every person, even those under 21 years old, has the right to refuse the test. If you refuse the test, your driver's license or learner's permit will automatically be suspended for 12 months. Further, the fact that you refused the test can later be used against you at a trial for driving under the influence. If you refuse the test, and the charge of driving under the influence is later dismissed or reduced, the State will return the learner's permit or driver's license to you.

The following charts *approximate* blood alcohol content for males and females based on body weight and number of drinks consumed in a one hour period. However, a number of other factors may affect your blood alcohol content, such as your age, metabolism, medications, speed of consumption, health issues, and the amount of food in your stomach and small intestine. In the calculation below, one drink is equivalent to one 12 oz. regular beer, 5 oz. of wine, or 1.5 oz. shot of hard liquor.

There is no "safe" amount to drink and still be able to drive without impairment. *The charts below show how little it takes (only one drink or less) to meet the DUI standard for persons under 21 years old in Georgia (.02 grams).*

## ◀)) *Pay Attention!*
**The best rule to follow is don't drink and drive!**

## BLOOD ALCOHOL PERCENTAGE LEVEL CHART FOR MALES

| Body Weight | Number of Drinks Consumed in One Hour | | | | |
|---|---|---|---|---|---|
| | 1 | 2 | 3 | 4 | 5 |
| 100 lbs | .04 | .08 | .11 | .15 | .19 |
| 120 lbs | .03 | .06 | .09 | .12 | .16 |
| 140 lbs | .03 | .05 | .08 | .11 | .13 |
| 160 lbs | .02 | .05 | .07 | .09 | .12 |
| 180 lbs | .02 | .04 | .06 | .08 | .11 |
| 200 lbs | .02 | .04 | .06 | .08 | .09 |

## BLOOD ALCOHOL PERCENTAGE LEVEL CHART FOR FEMALES

| Body Weight | Number of Drinks Consumed in One Hour | | | | |
|---|---|---|---|---|---|
| | 1 | 2 | 3 | 4 | 5 |
| 90 lbs | .05 | .10 | .15 | .20 | .25 |
| 100 lbs | .05 | .09 | .14 | .18 | .23 |
| 120 lbs | .04 | .08 | .11 | .15 | .19 |
| 140 lbs | .03 | .07 | .10 | .13 | .16 |
| 160 lbs | .03 | .06 | .09 | .11 | .14 |
| 180 lbs | .03 | .05 | .08 | .10 | .13 |

The above charts are found on the website of the National
Institute on Alcohol Abuse and Alcoholism
(http://pubs.niaaa.nih.gov/publications/niaaa-guide/descFig7.htm).

## OPEN CONTAINER VIOLATION

## ♀ Did You Know?

**DID YOU KNOW that a violation of the open container law occurs even if no one in the car has been drinking?**

(i) **A crime occurs when a driver or passenger of a motor vehicle possesses or has ready access to an open container of alcohol.**

An open container of alcohol means any open can or bottle or a bottle that has a broken seal or has contents partially removed.

All that is required is that the driver or passenger has access to an open container of alcohol. No one in the car has to be drinking. Also, the car does not have to be moving for this crime to occur.

> **EXAMPLE**
>
> *Person A is stopped by the police for speeding. The officer sees a bottle of bourbon in the passenger seat that has a broken seal. Even though Person A has not been drinking, Person A can be charged with an open container violation.*

**EXAMPLE**

*Person A is a passenger sitting in a stopped car in a parking lot. Person B comes over to the car and gives Person A a beer. They do not see a police officer who is watching the whole event. The officer can arrest Person A and the driver for an open container violation.*

*Type of crime:* Misdemeanor
*Punishment:* Up to 12 months imprisonment

# CHAPTER FOURTEEN
## *OTHER DRIVING VIOLATIONS*

### HOMICIDE BY VEHICLE

## ♀ *Did You Know?*

**DID YOU KNOW that you can be guilty of felony vehicular homicide without having any drugs or alcohol in your system?**

*One evening, two married couples, all young attorneys, had dinner at a restaurant and drove home together on a major road in Atlanta with many curves. Coming in the opposite direction was an 18 year old who was drag racing another vehicle. The 18 year old lost control of his car and struck the car with the young attorneys head-on. The impact instantly killed three of the attorneys: the driver and two of the passengers. One passenger miraculously escaped without serious physical injury. The wreck left two children without a father and two other children without a father or a mother.*

*Even though the 18 year old had no alcohol or drugs in his system, he was guilty of three counts of felony vehicular homicide because he was driving in a reckless manner when the accident occurred. He pled guilty and was sentenced to 15 years in the state prison.*

**(i) The felony crime of homicide by vehicle occurs when a person, without planning or intent, causes the death of another while doing any of the following:**

- **Passing a stopped school bus that is loading or unloading passengers**
- **Being involved in a hit and run accident**
- **Driving recklessly**
- **Driving under the influence of alcohol or drugs**
- **Fleeing or attempting to elude a police officer**

 *Punishment:* 3 to 15 years imprisonment for each person who is killed in the accident.

> **EXAMPLE**
>
> *Person A passes a stopped school bus that is unloading passengers and accidentally kills a child crossing the street. Person A is guilty of felony vehicular homicide.*

**(i) The misdemeanor crime of homicide by vehicle occurs when a person, without planning or intent, causes the death of another while committing any traffic offense other than the offenses listed for the felony crime of homicide by vehicle.**

 *Punishment:* Up to 12 months imprisonment

**EXAMPLE**
*Person A hits and kills a pedestrian while making an illegal left turn. Person A is guilty of misdemeanor vehicular homicide.*

## RECKLESS DRIVING

(i) **The crime of reckless driving occurs when a person drives a vehicle with reckless disregard for the safety of other people or property.**

**EXAMPLE**
*Person A is arrested for driving Person A's car at a high rate of speed at night without lights. Person A is guilty of reckless driving.*

*Type of crime:* Misdemeanor
*Punishment:* Up to 12 months imprisonment *and* 6-month suspension of learner's permit or driver's license for a person under 21 years old

## RACING ON HIGHWAYS AND STREETS

Have you ever been stopped at a red light, with your friend in the lane next to you, and the two of you rev your engines as if you are NASCAR drivers ready to start the race? Neither one of you actually intends to race down the street, but your friend burns rubber when the light changes. **Both** of you could be charged with racing and lose your license for 6 months.

**(i)** **The crime of racing on highways and streets occurs when a person races or drag races one or more cars on a street or highway.**

<u>Racing</u> means an attempt to out gain, out distance, prevent another vehicle from passing, or arrive first at a given destination.

<u>Drag racing</u> means:

- Two cars, side by side, with the drivers accelerating in an attempt to out distance each other
- One or more cars racing from point A to point B to compare speed or power of acceleration

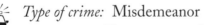 *Type of crime:* Misdemeanor
*Punishment:* Up to 12 months imprisonment *and* 6-month suspension of learner's permit or driver's license for a person under 21 years old

## AGGRESSIVE DRIVING

(i) **The crime of aggressive driving occurs when a person operates a motor vehicle with the intent to annoy, harass, intimidate, injure or obstruct another person.**

> ### EXAMPLE
> *Person A drives Person A's car just a few feet behind Person B's car for the purpose of annoying Person B. Person A is guilty of aggressive driving.*

*Type of crime:* Misdemeanor
*Punishment:* Up to 12 months imprisonment *and* 6-month suspension of learner's permit or driver's license for a person under 21 years old

## HIT-AND-RUN; LEAVING THE SCENE OF AN ACCIDENT

## ♀ Did You Know?
**DID YOU KNOW that you commit a crime if you leave the scene of a car accident?**

*A 16 year old was driving her parents' car when a child riding a bike darted out in front of the car and was struck and killed. The accident was unavoidable, and the driver of the car was in no way at fault. Unfortunately, in a state of panic, the driver fled the scene and went straight to her home instead of waiting for the police. Had she stayed at the scene of the accident, she would not have faced any charges. Because she left the scene, she was charged with felony hit-and-run.*

Leaving the scene of an accident only adds more problems. If you stay, you may find out that you were not at fault for the cause of the accident.

(i) **The crime of hit-and-run or leaving the scene of an accident occurs when a person involved in an accident resulting in injury to a person or damage to a vehicle fails to stop at the scene of the accident (or as close as possible to the accident) and fails to provide the following information:**
- **Name, address, and registration number of vehicle**
- **Driver's license, if requested**
- **Reasonable assistance to any injured person, including making arrangements for transporting a person to receive medical treatment**

*Type of crime: Felony* if the accident is the <u>proximate cause</u> of death or a serious injury; *misdemeanor* if the accident is the <u>proximate cause</u> of damage to vehicle or non-serious injury to person

*Punishment:* 1 to 5 years imprisonment for *felony*; up to 12 months imprisonment for *misdemeanor and* 6-month suspension of learner's permit or driver's license for a person under 21 years old

## STRIKING AN UNATTENDED VEHICLE

### ♀ *Did You Know?*

**DID YOU KNOW that you commit a crime if you strike a parked vehicle and fail to find the owner or leave a note?**

Have you ever parked your car in a parking lot and returned to find that someone had crunched your bumper or a door panel and did not leave you a note? If so, whoever hit your car just committed a crime.

ⓘ **A crime occurs when a person fails to notify the owner or operator of an unattended vehicle that the person strikes.**

*Type of crime:* Misdemeanor
*Punishment:* Up to 12 months imprisonment

## 🔊 *Pay Attention!*

*If you strike an unattended vehicle, try to locate the vehicle's operator or owner and notify that person of both your name and address and the name and address of your vehicle's owner.  Or, leave a note in an obvious place on the vehicle with your name and address and the name and address of your vehicle's owner.*

## ALLOWING A PERSON TO DRIVE WITHOUT A LICENSE

## 💡 *Did You Know?*

*DID YOU KNOW that you commit a crime if you let an unlicensed friend drive your car?*

I was the first person in my high school class to turn 16 and get a driver's license. Several of my friends who only had their learner's permit wanted me to let them drive my car.   I knew that if I got caught, my parents would not let me drive again for a very long time, so I refused, but the temptation was strong.

ⓘ *A crime occurs when a person allows an unlicensed driver to drive a motor vehicle owned by the person or under the person's control upon any highway, or a parent or guardian permits an unlicensed child under 18 years old to drive a motor vehicle on any highway.*

*Type of crime:* Misdemeanor
*Punishment:* Up to 12 months imprisonment

## UNLAWFUL DRIVING OF A PICK-UP TRUCK

(i) **A crime occurs when the driver of a pick-up truck allows a person under 18 years old to ride in the bed of the pick-up truck on an interstate highway.**

✗ **Exception:** If the bed of the pick-up truck is covered, there is no violation.

 *Type of crime:* Misdemeanor
*Punishment:* Up to 12 months imprisonment

## SUSPENSION OF A LEARNER'S PERMIT OR DRIVER'S LICENSE

### IF YOU ARE 15, 16, OR 17 YEARS OLD, YOUR LEARNER'S PERMIT OR DRIVER'S LICENSE MAY BE SUSPENDED:

1. If you drop out of school
2. If you accumulate 10 or more unexcused absences in the current academic year or the previous academic year

3. If you are found in violation by a school hearing officer, panel, or tribunal *or* have waived the right to a hearing and pled guilty to any of the following offenses:

  • threatening, striking, or causing bodily harm to a teacher or other school personnel
  • possession of alcohol on school property or at a school sponsored event
  • possession of marijuana or other drugs on school property or at a school sponsored event
  • sale of drugs or alcohol on school property or at a school sponsored event
  • possession or use of a weapon on school property or at a school sponsored event
  • any sexual offense
  • causing substantial physical or visible bodily harm to or seriously disfiguring another person, including a student

**Period of suspension for 1-3 above:** Until the first to occur of the following: 12 months after the date of suspension *or* your 18th birthday *or* when you have satisfactory proof that you are pursuing or have completed secondary education *or* when you enroll in a post-secondary school.

4. If you accumulate 4 or more driving points in a 12 month consecutive period.

**Period of Suspension for 4 above:** 6 months

**EXAMPLE**

*Person A received two speeding tickets for going 15 miles over the speed limit within 12 months. Person A will accumulate 4 points, and Person A's license will be suspended.*

## IF YOU ARE UNDER 21 YEARS OLD, YOUR LEARNER'S PERMIT OR DRIVER'S LICENSE MAY BE SUSPENDED:

1. If you are convicted of driving under the influenece of alcohol or drugs
2. If you refuse to submit to a breathalyzer or blood test when requested by a law enforcement officer who has reason to believe you are driving under the influence of alcohol

**Period of Suspension for 1-2 above:** 12 months, or 6 months if alcohol concentration is lower than .08

3. If you are convicted of a hit and run
4. If you are convicted of leaving the scene of an accident
5. If you are convicted of racing on highways or streets
6. If you are convicted of fleeing or attempting to elude a police officer while driving
7. If you are convicted of reckless driving
8. If you are convicted of exceeding the speed limit by 24 miles per hour or more
9. If you are convicted of purchasing an alcoholic beverage
10. If you are convicted of misrepresenting your age for the purpose of buying an alcoholic beverage

11. If you are convicted of possessing, selling, or distributing marijuana or other drugs
12. If you are convicted of driving offenses for which you receive 4 or more driving points

**Period of Suspension for 3-12 above:** 6 months

13. If you are convicted of Minor in Possession of alcohol

**Period of Suspension for 13 above:** 120 days

## ◀))  *Pay Attention!*

*A person who is under 21 years old and is driving with an alcohol concentration of .02 grams or greater is driving under the influence of alcohol.*

## ♀ *Did You Know?*

*DID YOU KNOW that even if an offense is in another state, your Georgia learner's permit or driver's license can be suspended?*

If you plead guilty to or are convicted of an offense in another state, and the offense is one that can result in suspension if it occurs in Georgia, the Department of Driver Services can suspend your Georgia learner's permit or driver's license.

# POINTS FOR SPEEDING AND OTHER DRIVING VIOLATIONS

If you are guilty of a driving violation, you will receive <u>driving points</u> on your personal motor vehicle record, with more serious violations receiving higher points. Driving points can increase the cost of your insurance, result in the suspension of your learner's permit or driver's license, and delay your ability to apply for a Class D driver's license (if you have a learner's permit) or a Class C driver's license (if you have a Class D driver's license).

If you are under 18 years old and accumulate 4 or more points in a 12 month period, or if you are under 21 years old and are guilty of a driving violation worth 4 points or more, your learner's permit or driver's license will be suspended.

The following is a partial list of the <u>assignment of points for certain driving violations</u>:
- Exceeding the speed limit by more than 14 mph, but less than 19 mph:     *2 points*
- Exceeding the speed limit by 19 mph, but less than 24 mph:     *3 points*
- Exceeding the speed limit by 24 mph, but less than 34 mph:     *4 points*
- Exceeding the speed limit by 34 mph or more:  *6 points*
- Aggressive driving:  *6 points*
- Reckless driving:  *4 points*
- Unlawful passing of a school bus:  *6 points*
- Improper passing on a hill or curve:  *4 points*

# CHAPTER FIFTEEN
## AGE OF CONSENT AND STATUTORY RAPE

### ♀ Did You Know?

**DID YOU KNOW that you can be charged with statutory rape even if the other person tells you he or she is 16 years old?**

**And.....DID YOU KNOW that you can be charged with statutory rape even if the other person under 16 years old consents to have sex?**

*A 17 year old male honor student at a local high school met the female cousin of one of his neighbors during summer vacation. The cousin was staying in town for several weeks. She told the boy she was 16 years old. He had no reason not to believe her because she looked 16, and she was in the same grade. (She was actually only 15 years old.) They dated several times during the summer and had sexual intercourse.*

*When the girl went back to her home in another Georgia city, the girl and the boy both started back to school in their own high schools. One morning, the girl's mother accidentally found her daughter's diary, and she read about her daughter's summer romance. (The girl did not leave out any detail!) The mother told her husband, and they both drove to the boy's town and got a judge to issue a warrant for the boy's arrest for statutory rape. He was arrested at his home and taken off to jail in handcuffs, where he was locked up with the other adult prisoners.*

*Even though the boy believed his girlfriend was 16, he was still guilty of statutory rape because she was actually only 15 at the time they had sex.*

The legal age for consent to sexual contact in Georgia is 16 years old.

The age of consent for sexual contact in Georgia used to be 14 years old. That is, as long as the person was 14 years old or older, and he or she consented to the sexual contact, in most cases the sexual contact was not a crime. In 1995, the legislature raised the age of consent to 16 years old. When that happened, more teenagers were charged with sex crimes.

<u>Sexual contact</u> means **any** type of sexual activity, including touching of the other person's breasts or sexual organs or buttocks, oral sex, or sexual intercourse.

 **The crime of statutory rape occurs when a person has sexual intercourse with a person under 16 years old.**

## ⚲ *Did You Know?*
**DID YOU KNOW that you can be charged with statutory rape regardless of whether you are a girl or a boy?**

Statutory rape, unlike rape, is gender neutral. A male or a female can be either a victim or a perpetrator of statutory rape. Consent (permission and willingness) to sexual intercourse is irrelevant.

*Type of crime:* Felony
*Punishment:* 1 to 20 years imprisonment

**✗ Exception:** If the defendant is over 21 years old, the defendant must serve at least 10 years in prison *without parole* and can be sentenced up to 20 years in prison *without parole.*

**✗ Romeo and Juliet Exception:** The legislature passed what is known as the "Romeo and Juliet" exception to the punishment for statutory rape. If the victim is at least 14 years old, and the defendant is 18 years old or younger and is no more than 4 years older than the victim, then the crime is a **misdemeanor**, and the punishment is up to 12 months in prison. Even though the punishment is a misdemeanor, statutory rape is still a crime, and if you are 17 years old or older, this crime will be part of your criminal history record for the rest of your life.

> ### EXAMPLE
> *Person A is 16 years old and has sexual intercourse with Person B who is 15 years old. Person A is guilty of misdemeanor statutory rape, and, due to the age of Person A, will be prosecuted in juvenile court.*

**EXAMPLE**

*Person A and Person B are both 15 years old and have sexual intercourse. Person A and Person B are both guilty of misdemeanor statutory rape, and, due to the ages of Person A and Person B, will be prosecuted in juvenile court.*

**EXAMPLE**

*Person A is 20 years old, and Person B is 15 years old. Person A and Person B have sexual intercourse. Person A is guilty of felony statutory rape, with punishment of 1 to 20 years in prison.*

# CHAPTER SIXTEEN
## SEX CRIMES WITH FORCE

## RAPE

### ℗ Did You Know?
**DID YOU KNOW that you commit rape if you have sex with someone who is too intoxicated to give her consent?**

*An 18 year old college freshman went to a fraternity party where she drank "hunch-punch" that contained grain alcohol. She does not remember much of what happened later that evening, but she awoke the next morning in someone else's bed, unclothed, feeling sick, with a guy next to her whom she did not remember. She could tell that at some point she had had sex the night before, but she did not remember doing it. She went back to her dorm and told her roommate, and they went to a rape crisis clinic where she told her story to a counselor. The police were called, and the boy she found in bed with her was arrested for rape.*

ⓘ **The crime of rape occurs when a male forces a female to have sexual intercourse against her will.**

Sexual intercourse with a female under 10 years old is automatically rape; "force" and "against her will" do not need to be proven.

Only a male can be convicted of the crime of rape.

Force does not require a weapon. Force does not require actual physical injury to the female. Fear and intimidation may be all that is necessary to show force.

## ◀))  Pay Attention!

**"Against her will" does not require the female to say "no." She can show her refusal by any means necessary to show she does not want to engage in sexual intercourse.**

If a female is so intoxicated by alcohol or drugs that she is incapable of giving consent, then "force" and "against her will" are assumed to be proven.

## ◀))  Pay Attention!

**If you believe you have been a victim of rape, do not bathe or wash clothes, and report the rape immediately to the police or a rape crisis center.**

*Type of crime:* Felony
*Punishment:* Life *without parole or* life in prison *or* a minimum of 25 years in prison *without parole*

## ◀⟩) *Pay Attention!*

*Rape is one of the seven deadly sins. A person 13, 14, 15, or 16 years old when the crime was committed can be prosecuted and punished as an adult for the crime of rape.*

## AGGRAVATED SODOMY

(i) *The crime of aggravated sodomy occurs when a person forces another person against the other person's will to engage in sodomy.*

<u>Sodomy</u> is oral sex or anal sex. Aggravated sodomy is similar to the crime of rape, but rape involves sexual intercourse, and aggravated sodomy involves oral or anal sex.

Unlike the crime of rape, aggravated sodomy is gender neutral. A male or a female can be a victim or a perpetrator of aggravated sodomy.

Sodomy with a person under 10 years old is automatically aggravated sodomy; "force" and "against the person's will" do not need to be proven.

*Type of crime:* Felony
*Punishment:* Minimum of 25 years in prison *without parole* to life in prison.

## ◀)) *Pay Attention!*

*Aggravated sodomy is one of the seven deadly sins. A person 13, 14, 15, or 16 years old when the crime was committed may be prosecuted and punished as an adult for aggravated sodomy.*

## SEXUAL BATTERY

## ♀ *Did You Know?*

*DID YOU KNOW that you can be charged with sexual battery for touching your classmates on their butts?*

*As two middle school boys walked down the hall between classes, they both squeezed the butts of female classmates. Both boys were arrested for sexual battery.*

(i) *The crime of sexual battery occurs when a person touches the genital area, groin, inner thighs, anus, buttocks, or female breasts without the other person's consent.*

Touching outer clothing in these areas can be sexual battery; skin contact is not required.

Sexual battery is gender neutral. A male or a female can be a victim or a perpetrator of sexual battery.

*Type of crime:* Misdemeanor
*Punishment:* Up to 12 months imprisonment

## ◄))) *Pay Attention!*

*If the victim is under 16 years old, the crime is a felony, and the punishment is 1 to 5 years imprisonment.*

## AGGRAVATED SEXUAL BATTERY

(i) *The crime of aggravated sexual battery occurs when a person inserts anything other than a penis into the vagina or anus of another person without the other person's consent.*

> **EXAMPLE**
> *Person A inserts Person A's finger into the vagina of Person B without Person B's consent. Person A is guilty of aggravated sexual battery.*

*Type of crime:* Felony
*Punishment:* Minimum of 25 years in prison *without parole* to life in prison.

Aggravated sexual battery is gender neutral. A male or a female can be a victim or a perpetrator of aggravated sexual battery.

### 🔊 *Pay Attention!*

*Aggravated sexual battery is one of the seven deadly sins. A person 13, 14, 15, or 16 years old when the crime was committed can be prosecuted and punished as an adult for aggravated sexual battery.*

# CHAPTER SEVENTEEN
## SEX CRIMES AGAINST CHILDREN

Most sex crimes against children involve older adults and children. In almost every case, a child reports the case long after the abuse occurs. In fact, in many cases, the abuse occurs several times before the child tells anyone.

One of the purposes of this book is to educate you regarding crimes against children and to encourage you to report if you know anyone who is being abused by an adult.

## CHILD MOLESTATION

(i) *The crime of child molestation occurs when a person commits "any immoral or indecent act" to, or in the presence of, or with any child under 16 years old with the intent to arouse the sexual desires of either the child or the person.*

"Immoral or indecent acts" is a broad term. The jury has wide discretion in determining what are "immoral and indecent acts."

Child molestation does not require sexual intercourse or sodomy. The mere touching of a child for sexual gratification or to arouse the sexual desires of a child can be child molestation.

Child molestation does not require physical touching of a child. Masturbation in the presence of a child is child molestation.

Child molestation is gender neutral. A male or a female can be a victim or a perpetrator of child molestation.

*Type of crime:* Felony
*Punishment:* 5 to 20 years imprisonment

**✗ Romeo and Juliet Exception:** If the victim is at least 14 years old but less than 16 years old, and the defendant is 18 years old or younger and no more than 4 years older than the victim, the defendant is guilty of a misdemeanor, and the punishment is up to 12 months imprisonment.

**EXAMPLE**
*Person A is 18 years old, and Person B is 15 years old. Person A places Person A's hands on the breasts of Person B. Person A is guilty of child molestation (misdemeanor), even if Person B consents to the touching.*

**EXAMPLE**
*Person A is 18 years old, and Person B is 13 years old. Person A places Person A's hands on the breasts of Person B. Person A is guilty of child molestation (felony), even if Person B consents to the touching.*

# AGGRAVATED CHILD MOLESTATION

ⓘ *The crime of aggravated child molestation occurs when a person 1) physically injures a child while committing the act of child molestation, or 2) commits an act of sodomy (oral or anal sex) with a person under 16 years old.*

*A case involving a Georgia teenager has made local and national news. In that case, a 17 year old engaged in oral sex with a 15 year old. The jury found the teenager not guilty of rape but found him guilty of aggravated child molestation because the girl was only 15 years old when they had oral sex. Because the "Romeo and Juliet" exception had not passed the legislature at the time the crime occurred, he was sentenced to the mandatory minimum amount of 10 years in prison. Today, with the Romeo and Juliet exception, he would be prosecuted for a misdemeanor and could receive a sentence of up to 12 months. Even if the teenager had been convicted of a misdemeanor, the crime of aggravated child molestation would still be part of his criminal history record for the rest of his life.*

Like child molestation, aggravated child molestation is gender neutral. A male or a female can be a victim or a perpetrator.

*Type of crime:* Felony
*Punishment:* Minimum of 25 years imprisonment *without parole* to life in prison

**✗ Romeo and Juliet Exception:** If the victim is at least 14 years old but less than 16 years old, and the defendant is 18 years old or younger and no more than 4 years older than the victim, the crime is a misdemeanor, and the punishment is up to 12 months imprisonment.

## 📢 *Pay Attention!*

*Aggravated child molestation is one of the seven deadly sins. Persons 13, 14, 15, and 16 years old when the crime is committed can be prosecuted and punished as an adult, even if the crime is a misdemeanor.*

> ### EXAMPLE
>
> *Person A is 16 years old and has oral sex with Person B who is 15 years old. Person A is guilty of aggravated child molestation and can be prosecuted and punished as an adult, even if Person B consents to the oral sex. Because of the ages of Person A and Person B, the crime is a misdemeanor. Person A can receive up to 12 months in jail.*

## ENTICING A CHILD FOR INDECENT PURPOSES

ⓘ *The crime of enticing a child for indecent purposes occurs when a person solicits, entices, or takes any person under 16 years old to any place for the purpose of child molestation or indecent acts.*

"Indecent acts" is a broad term. The jury has wide discretion in determining what are "indecent acts."

The person under 16 years old does not actually have to be taken to a place. All that is required is that the person be solicited or enticed to go some place for the purpose of child molestation or an indecent act.

> **EXAMPLE**
> *Person A invites Person B, who is 15 years old, to Person A's house for the purpose of taking nude pictures of Person B. Person B does not go to Person A's house. Person A is guilty of enticing a child for indecent purposes, even if Person B never goes to Person A's house.*

*Type of crime:* Felony
*Punishment:* Minimum of 10 years imprisonment *without parole* to 30 years in prison *without parole*

✗ **Romeo and Juliet Exception:** If the victim is at least 14 years old but less than 16 years old, and the defendant is 18 years old or younger and no more than 4 years older than the victim, the crime is a misdemeanor, and the punishment is up to 12 months imprisonment.

# SEXUAL ASSAULT AGAINST A STUDENT BY SCHOOL OFFICIALS

*A 17 year old high school football player bragged to his fellow teammates that he was having sex with one of his teachers. A teammate told his parents what he heard, and the parents called the police. The teacher was arrested for sexual assault by a school official. Even though the student was above the age of consent (16 years old), the teacher still committed a crime because she was the student's teacher.*

Georgia law provides protection for certain persons because of their status with another person. Persons in a position of power cannot use their position to take advantage of another person. For this reason, teachers and principals cannot have any type of sexual contact with a student.

(i) **A crime occurs when a custodian or a supervisor of a student (such as a teacher or a principal) has sexual contact with a student for sexual gratification.**

Any touching of a student's genital area, inner thighs, breasts, or buttocks may be a violation of this law. Touching outer clothing in these areas is child molestation. Sexual intercourse and skin contact are not required.

*Type of crime:* Felony
*Punishment:* Minimum of 10 years in prison *without parole* to 30 years in prison *without parole*

**✗ Exception:** If the student is younger then 14 years old, the school teacher or principal must serve at least 25 years in prison *without parole.*

## SEXUAL EXPLOITATION OF PERSONS UNDER 18 YEARS OLD (CHILD PORNOGRAPHY)

ⓘ *The crime of sexual exploitation of persons under 18 years old (child pornography) occurs in any of the following situations:*

1. *A person persuades or forces a person under 18 years old to expose genitals or pubic area or engage in actual or simulated sexually explicit conduct for the purpose of photographing or making a video recording showing such conduct.*
2. *A person possesses or distributes any photograph or video recording showing sexual conduct described above.*
3. *A parent or guardian permits a child under 18 years old to engage in sexual conduct described above.*

*Type of crime:* Felony
*Punishment:* 5 to 20 years imprisonment

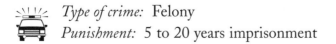

## ♀ *Did You Know?*

**DID YOU KNOW that there is no Romeo and Juliet exception for taking sexually explicit photographs or videos? If you take sexually explicit photographs or videotapes of a person under 18 years old, you commit a felony.**

*A 17 year old boy went to the home of his 15 year old girl friend. (She was just a couple weeks short of being 16 years old at the time.) No one else was home, and they went to her bedroom where they made a video of the two of them performing various sexual acts. They misplaced the video, and the girl's little sister found the tape and gave it to her parents.*

*The boy was arrested for statutory rape, aggravated child molestation, and sexual exploitation of a child. All of these crimes were felonies at that time.*

Today, under the Romeo and Juliet exception, the first two charges, statutory rape and aggravated child molestation, are misdemeanors, but the boy would still have to be prosecuted as an adult for those crimes because of his age (17 years old). The third charge, child exploitation, is still a felony even with only a two-year difference between the boy and the girl.

*A 17 year old took a picture of his nude 17 year old girlfriend with his cell phone. He sent the picture to one of his friends. The 17 year old boy was charged with distributing child pornography, a felony.*

## COMPUTER SOLICITATION OF MINORS FOR SEX

 *The crime of computer solicitation of minors for sex occurs if:*

- *A person uses a computer to offer or solicit sex with a person under 16 years old or to offer or solicit a picture or video of a child engaged in sexually explicit conduct.*
- *A person has contact via the use of a computer with a minor under 16 years old or someone the person thinks is under 16 years old, and such contact includes sexually explicit language for the purpose of arousing the sexual desires of the person or the minor.*

*Type of crime:* Felony
*Punishment:* 1 to 20 years imprisonment

**✕ Romeo and Juliet Exception:** If the victim is 14 or 15 years old, and the defendant is no more then 3 years older than the victim, the crime is a misdemeanor, and the punishment is up to 12 months imprisonment.

**EXAMPLE**

*Person A is 17 years old, and Person B is 15 years old. Person A sends an e-mail to Person B suggesting that they get together for sex. Person A is guilty of computer solicitation of sex with a minor. Because of the Romeo and Juliet exception, the crime is a misdemeanor.*

**EXAMPLE**

*A 15 year old receives an e-mail from an adult with pornographic pictures and sexually explicit language. The 15 year old reports the incident to a parent, who contacts the police. The adult is charged with computer solicitation of sex with a minor, a felony.*

## REPORTING CHILD ABUSE

Georgia law requires that certain professionals report to the authorities any time they have a reason to believe that a person under 18 years old is a victim of sexual abuse, physical abuse, mental abuse, or neglect.

The persons who are required to report child abuse include doctors, hospital or medical personnel, dentists, psychologists, podiatrists, nurses, social workers, family therapists, school teachers, school administrators, child welfare agency personnel, child counselors, persons who work for agencies that provide services to children (such as the YMCA), and law enforcement. *The failure to report child abuse by any person listed is a misdemeanor.*

*If a person required by law to report child abuse has a reasonable cause to believe that a child has been abused, the person must immediately report the abuse.* The report may be made to the Department of Family and Children Services, the police, or the district attorney. After making an oral report, a reporting person may be asked to provide a written report. The reporting person should keep a copy of the report to verify that a report was made regarding the abuse.

Other persons may report child abuse if they have a reason to believe a child is being abused. You may wonder if someone has the right to sue you if you report child abuse. The answer is no, if a report of child abuse is made in good faith.

A common question is whether a person should report child abuse if the person learns that a child was abused in the past, but is not currently being abused. *Because the deadline under the law for reporting most crimes of child abuse is seven years after the victim's 16th birthday, the best practice is to report the abuse.*

If you have been abused or know someone who has been abused, you can contact the **Prevent Child Abuse Georgia** helpline toll-free at 1-800-CHILDREN (1-800-244-5373) or by e-mail to helpline@pcageorgia.org. All calls made to the Helpline are confidential.

Reports of child abuse are confidential. However, if a criminal prosecution or lawsuit results from a report, the contents of the report may be disclosed, including the name of the person who made the report.

# CHAPTER EIGHTEEN
## OTHER CRIMES AGAINST CHILDREN

### CONTRIBUTING TO THE DELINQUENCY OF A MINOR

*Following a high school graduation, a mother of one of the graduates hosted a party at her home and provided beer to her son's classmates. She was arrested and charged with multiple counts of contributing to the delinquency of a minor — one count for each teenager who was provided alcohol.*

ⓘ **The crime of contributing to the delinquency, unruliness, or deprivation of a minor (under 17 years old) occurs when a person knowingly and willfully:**
- **Helps or encourages a minor to be an unruly child**
- **Helps or encourages a minor in committing a delinquent act**
- **Commits an act, or fails to act, so that the minor is found to be a deprived child**
- **Provides a minor with a weapon for the purpose of committing a crime that involves force or violence**
- **Hires or encourages any minor to commit a felony that involves force or violence as part of the crime.**

In the last two situations, the minor does not actually have to commit the crime.

*Type of crime: Misdemeanor* for the first three acts described above; *felony* for the last two acts described above
*Punishment:* Up to 12 months imprisonment for *misdemeanor*, 1 to 5 years imprisonment for *felony*

**✗ Exception:**  If the third act described above results in serious injury or death to a child, the crime will be a felony, and the punishment will be 1 to 5 years imprisonment.

> **EXAMPLE**
> *Person A encourages Person B, who is 15 years old, to commit the crime of shoplifting.  Person A is guilty of contributing to the delinquency of a minor.*

> **EXAMPLE**
> *Person A does not make Person A's son go to school. Person A's son is 14 years old and has no health reason for missing school. Person A is guilty of contributing to the deprivation of a minor.*

> **EXAMPLE**
> *Person A encourages Person B, who is 16 years old, to commit the crime of aggravated assault on another person. Even if Person B does not commit the aggravated assault, Person A is guilty of contributing to the delinquency of a minor.*

# ॰ *Did You Know?*

**DID YOU KNOW that a teenager can be guilty of contributing to the delinquency of a minor?**

**EXAMPLE**

*Person A is 17 years old, and Person B is 16 years old. Person A gives alcohol to Person B, who dies from alcohol intoxication. Person A is guilty of a felony.*

## CRUELTY TO CHILDREN (PHYSICAL OR MENTAL ABUSE OR NEGLECT)

Unfortunately, I prosecuted a number of cases of cruelty to children (physical or mental child abuse or neglect). Some of these cases involved the excessive beating of a child where the child almost died from the beating; failure to provide medical attention to a child where the child had been injured by a parent's boyfriend; and locking a child in a closet for several days. If you know or suspect that a child is a victim of child abuse, you should contact the police or the Prevent Child Abuse Georgia Helpline at 1-800-CHILDREN (1-800-244-5373) or by e-mail to helpline@pcageorgia.org.

Unlike most crimes in Georgia, the crime of Cruelty to Children has different degrees of severity.

(i) **The crime of cruelty to children in the first degree occurs in either of the following situations:**

- **A person maliciously causes a child under 18 years old cruel or excessive physical or mental pain.**

**EXAMPLE**

*Person A whips a child for several hours while using abusive language. Person A is guilty of Cruelty to Children in the first degree.*

**EXAMPLE**

*Person A does not take Person A's child to the doctor for medical treatment after the child is severely injured by Person A's friend. Person A is guilty of Cruelty to Children in the first degree.*

**EXAMPLE**

*Person A murders Person B, who is Person A's spouse. One of their kids witnesses the murder. Person A is guilty of Murder and Cruelty to Children in the first degree.*

- **A parent, guardian, or other person supervising the welfare of a child under 18 years old or having immediate custody or charge of a child under 18 years old willfully deprives the child of necessary sustenance to the extent that the child's health or well-being is jeopardized.**

Sustenance means necessary food or drink sufficient to support life and maintain health.

**EXAMPLE**

*Person A fails to provide baby formula for Person A's child. Person A's child becomes severely malnourished. Person A is guilty of Cruelty to Children in the first degree.*

 *Type of crime:* Felony
*Punishment:* 5 to 20 years imprisonment

(i) **The crime of cruelty to children in the second degree occurs when a person, because of criminal negligence, causes a child under 18 years old cruel or excessive physical or mental pain.**

<u>Criminal negligence</u> means an act or failure to act with a willful or reckless disregard for the safety of others who might reasonably be expected to be injured because of the act or failure to act.

**EXAMPLE**

*Person A knowingly leaves a loaded firearm in the presence of Person B who is 10 years old. Person B shoots the gun which causes injury to Person B. Person A is guilty of Cruelty to Children in the second degree.*

 *Type of crime:* Felony
*Punishment:* 1 to 10 years imprisonment

**ⓘ** **The crime of cruelty to children in the third degree occurs when a person, who is the primary aggressor, intentionally allows a child under 18 years old to witness or hear a forcible felony, or a battery, or an act of family violence.**

Knowledge that a child under 18 years old is present is sufficient.

 *Type of crime:* Misdemeanor
*Punishment:* Up to 12 months imprisonment

> **EXAMPLE**
> *Person A strikes Person B. Person B's child is in the room and can see or hear Person B being hit. Person A is guilty of misdemeanor Cruelty to Children in the third degree.*

# CHAPTER NINETEEN
## ASSAULT AND BATTERY

My experience has shown that teenagers get into trouble with crimes such as assault and battery primarily for two reasons: 1) they lose their temper and do not think about the consequences of their actions, or 2) they are goaded by their friends into doing something stupid, such as firing a gun at someone's house. Keep your cool (counting to 10 really does work), and remember that "they made me do it" is not a defense to a crime!

## SIMPLE ASSAULT

### ♀ Did You Know?
**DID YOU KNOW that threatening someone with violence might be enough to charge you with simple assault?**

*Following a high school baseball game, one of the players believed that a teammate had stolen his watch. He raised his fist and told his teammate to return his watch, or he was going to hit the teammate. Although he never hit his teammate, and he never intended to hit his teammate, he was still guilty of a simple assault because he threatened his teammate with a violent injury.*

(i) **The crime of simple assault occurs when a person:**

- **Attempts to commit a violent injury toward another person, or**
- **Commits an act that places another person in reasonable apprehension of immediately receiving a violent injury**

The aggressor does not actually have to harm or even intend to harm the other person. A crime occurs if the other person reasonably believes harm is about to happen.

*Type of crime:* Misdemeanor
*Punishment:* Up to 12 months imprisonment

## AGGRAVATED ASSAULT

### ♀ Did You Know?

**DID YOU KNOW that threatening someone with any object that can cause serious bodily injury is a felony and that you can be sentenced up to 20 years in prison if you are 17 years old or older?**

*A 17 year old was given a gun by a gang member. His friends told him to find a rival gang member, put the gun to his head, and tell the other gang member that he has to move out of the neighborhood. The 17 year old followed these instructions. Even though he never pulled the trigger, the 17 year old was guilty of aggravated assault with a firearm.*

(i) **The crime of aggravated assault occurs when a person:**

- **Assaults another person with the intent (purpose) to murder, rape, or rob the other person**
- **Assaults another person with a deadly weapon, such as a knife or gun**
- **Assaults another person with an object that can cause serious bodily injury or death (such as a baseball bat, belt, shoe, car, or other everyday item not normally considered a weapon)**
- **Fires a gun from within a motor vehicle toward another person. The victim does not have to have knowledge that a person in a car fired a gun toward the victim.**

**EXAMPLE**

*Person A believes that Person B stole Person A's book bag. Person A tries to hit Person B with a metal pipe, but Person B ducks, and Person A never makes contact with Person B. Person A is guilty of aggravated assault.*

**EXAMPLE**

*Person A assaults Person B with the intent to rape Person B. Person B is able to free herself and get away before Person A can have sex with Person B. Person A is guilty of aggravated assault.*

**EXAMPLE**

*Person A, while inside a car, fires a gun at Person B. The bullet misses Person B. Person B did not even know at the time that Person B was a target. Person A is guilty of aggravated assault.*

*Type of Crime:* Felony
*Punishment:* 1 to 20 years imprisonment

## 📢 *Pay Attention!*

**The punishment increases to 5 to 20 years in prison if the victim is:**

- **a law enforcement officer**
- **a student, teacher, or other school personnel, and the assault occurs within a school safety zone**

## 📢 *Pay Attention!*

**The punishment is 25 to 50 years imprisonment without parole if the victim is under 14 years old, and the assault is with the intent to rape.**

## SIMPLE BATTERY

**The crime of simple battery occurs when a person intentionally:**

- **Causes physical harm to another person, or**
- **Makes physical contact of an insulting or provoking nature with another person**

**EXAMPLE**

*Person A intentionally grabs Person B's wrist and twists Person B's arm behind Person B's back. As a result, Person B suffers a sprained wrist. Person A is guilty of simple battery.*

 *Type of crime:* Misdemeanor
*Punishment:* Up to 12 months imprisonment

## BATTERY

(i) **The crime of battery occurs when a person intentionally:**
- **Causes substantial physical harm to another, or**
- **Causes visible bodily harm to another**

Visible bodily harm may include injuries such as blackened eyes, swollen lips, or substantial bruises.

✗ **Exception:** A parent is not guilty of battery on a child if the parent is administering reasonable corporal punishment on a child.

**EXAMPLE**

*Person A is mad at Person B. Person A walks up to Person B and punches Person B in the eye. As a result, Person B suffers a black eye. Person A is guilty of battery.*

**EXAMPLE**

*Person A gives Person A's child a spanking for misbehaving. The spanking leaves Person A's handprint on the child's buttocks but does not cause severe bruising. Person A is not guilty of battery.*

*Type of crime:* Misdemeanor
*Punishment:* Up to 12 months imprisonment

## ◁))  *Pay Attention!*

**Battery against a teacher or other school personnel engaged in official duties or on school property is a felony, and the punishment is 1 to 5 years imprisonment.**

## AGGRAVATED BATTERY

ⓘ  **The crime of aggravated battery occurs when a person maliciously causes bodily harm to another by:**
- **Depriving the other person of a body part (such as an arm, leg, or eye)**
- **Rendering a body part of the other person useless**
- **Seriously disfiguring the other person's body**

The deprivation of a body part does not need to be permanent.

**EXAMPLE**

*During a pick-up baseball game, a player who is at bat is hit by a wild pitch. The player angrily races toward the pitcher's mound, swings the bat, and breaks the pitcher's arm. The player is charged with aggravated battery.*

*Type of crime:* Felony
*Punishment:* 1 to 20 years imprisonment

## 📢 *Pay Attention!*

**The punishment will be 5 to 20 years imprisonment if the victim is a student, teacher or other school personnel, and the aggravated battery occurs in a school safety zone. The punishment will be 10 to 20 years imprisonment if the aggravated battery is against a law enforcement official who is on duty when the aggravated battery occurs.**

## OBSTRUCTION OF A POLICE OFFICER

**ⓘ A crime occurs when a person hinders or obstructs a law enforcement officer in the lawful discharge of the officer's official duties.**

*Type of crime:* Misdemeanor
*Punishment:* Up to 12 months imprisonment

## 📣 *Pay Attention!*

**If an act of violence is committed against a police officer, the crime is a felony, and the punishment is 1 to 5 years imprisonment.**

> **EXAMPLE**
>
> *A police officer arrives at a party where there is underage drinking and approaches Person A for questioning. Person A starts to run from the officer instead of answering any questions. Person A is guilty of obstruction of a police officer.*

## TERRORISTIC THREATS

## 🔎 *Did You Know?*

**DID YOU KNOW that it is a crime to threaten to do violence against another person if the threat is recorded or heard by someone else?**

*Two teenagers were having a dispute over a girlfriend. One of the boys called the other boy and left a voice message stating, "If you don't quit messin' with my girl I am going to kill you!" He was arrested for terroristic threats.*

ⓘ **The crime of terroristic threats occurs when a person threatens to commit any crime of violence against another person which is recorded or heard by a third party.**

*Type of Crime*: Felony
*Punishment*: 1 to 5 years imprisonment

## STALKING

*An 18 year old college freshman broke up with her high school boyfriend while she was away at school. When she came home for winter break, her former boyfriend started harassing her by leaving numerous voice mails on her cell phone. He also parked his car in front of her home. She asked him to leave her alone, to stop leaving her phone messages, and not to follow her. One evening she came home with a date, and her former boyfriend jumped from the bushes and attacked her date. He was arrested for stalking and battery.*

(i) **The crime of stalking occurs when a person follows, places under surveillance, or contacts another person for the purpose of harassing and intimidating the other person.**

*Type of Crime*: Misdemeanor
*Punishment*: Up to 12 months in prison

### ◀») *Pay Attention!*
*If you believe you are a victim of stalking, immediately tell your parents, guardian, or trusted adult. If the stalker does not stop the behavior, notify the police immediately before someone gets physically injured.*

# CHAPTER TWENTY
## ROBBERY AND ARMED ROBBERY

*A 14 year old middle school student took a 9mm handgun to school. Between classes, he pulled the gun from his book bag, stuck it in the mouth of a 13 year old classmate, and demanded that the 13 year old give him his sneakers. The 13 year old gave the 14 year old his sneakers, and the 14 year old went on to his class. The 13 year old reported the incident to his teacher, and the 14 year old was arrested. The 14 year old was prosecuted as an adult and received 15 years in prison <u>without parole</u>. The 13 year old was terrified to go back to school, and his parents had to move to another county so that he could feel safe again.*

## ROBBERY

ⓘ **The crime of robbery occurs when a person takes property belonging to another person, and in the immediate presence of another person, by any of the following:**
- **Use of force**
- **Fear or intimidation**
- **Sudden snatching**

**EXAMPLE**

*Person A grabs and takes a purse from Person B who is holding the purse waiting to cross the street. Person A is guilty of robbery.*

**EXAMPLE**

*Person A tells Person B that if Person B does not give Person B's bicycle to Person A, Person A will beat Person B up. Person B gives Person A the bicycle. Person A is guilty of robbery.*

*Type of crime:* Felony
*Punishment:* 1 to 20 years imprisonment

## ARMED ROBBERY

After the laws changed requiring that persons 13-16 years old be prosecuted as adults for certain crimes, the number of young people serving adult sentences significantly increased. Most of this increase was due to convictions involving armed robbery. The 13-16 year old was often not the person holding the gun but was with the person who actually had the gun and who demanded money or other property, like a vehicle. However, any person who participates in an armed robbery is just as guilty as the person holding the gun. (See Parties to a Crime, Chapter Four)

Teenagers rarely act alone to commit an armed robbery. Unfortunately, if you are in a group that commits an armed robbery, you could end up spending, at a minimum, a decade in prison.

## ⚲ *Did You Know?*

**DID YOU KNOW that if you participate in an armed robbery, you can be guilty of armed robbery even if you don't hold the weapon?**

ⓘ **The crime of armed robbery occurs when a person takes the property of another person:**
- **While using an offensive weapon; or**
- **With something that looks like an offensive weapon**

The weapon does not have to be a firearm; it can be any weapon that can cause death or serious bodily injury to another person.

> **EXAMPLE**
> *Person A, while holding a knife, takes Person B's purse away from Person B. Person A is guilty of armed robbery.*

*Type of crime:* Felony
*Punishment:* Minimum of 10 years *without parole* up to 20 years or life in prison

### ◀))  *Pay Attention!*

*Armed robbery is one of the seven deadly sins.  A person 13-16 years old when the crime was committed can be prosecuted and punished as an adult for the crime of armed robbery if committed with a firearm.*

# CHAPTER TWENTY-ONE
## *TAKING ANOTHER PERSON'S LIFE*

*Two boys, ages 14 and 16, attended the same high school, but they did not know each other. One day when passing each other in the hall, one boy bumped the other boy, and words were exchanged. Instead of just passing it off and walking on to class, they immediately decided to go outside and fight. The 16 year old tried to walk away from the fight, but the other students goaded him into staying and fighting. When he approached the 14 year old, the 14 year old pulled out a knife and lunged at the 16 year old, stabbing him in the heart. He died two minutes later on the playground.*

*Two boys' lives were instantly destroyed that fateful day. The 14 year old was prosecuted as an adult. Because he had a knife on school grounds, a felony, and because someone died as a result of his having the knife, he was found guilty of felony murder and sentenced to mandatory life in prison.*

## MURDER AND FELONY MURDER

 ***The crime of murder occurs when a person takes the life of another person with malice aforethought.***

<u>Malice aforethought</u> means the deliberate intention to take the life of another person without justification, such as self-defense. Murder does not require premeditation. The intent to take another person's life can be formed instantly and at the same time as the killing.

> **EXAMPLE**
>
> *Person A gets into an argument with Person B and decides during the argument to shoot Person B. Person B dies from the gunshot wound. If Person B did nothing to cause Person A to be in fear of Person A's life, Person A is guilty of murder.*

(i) **The crime of felony murder occurs when, while a person is committing a felony crime, another person is killed, usually accidentally.**

> **EXAMPLE**
>
> *Person A, while robbing a store at gunpoint, accidentally drops the gun. The gun fires and kills a bystander. Person A is guilty of felony murder.*

*Type of crime:* Felony
*Punishment:* Life in prison with the possibility of parole after first serving 25 years in prison *or* life *without parole or* death.

## 📢 **Pay Attention!**

**Murder/felony murder is one of the seven deadly sins. A person 13-16 years old when the crime was committed can be prosecuted and punished as an adult for the crime of murder or felony murder but cannot receive the death penalty.**

## VOLUNTARY MANSLAUGHTER

ⓘ *The crime of voluntary manslaughter occurs when a person takes the life of another person as a result of a sudden, violent, irresistible passion resulting from being seriously provoked by the other person in a manner sufficient to provoke a reasonable person.*

If there is a "cooling off" period between the time of being provoked and the killing, the crime will be murder instead of voluntary manslaughter.

Mere words by the other person cannot be enough to provoke someone to commit voluntary manslaughter.

> **EXAMPLE**
> *Person A finds Person A's girlfriend in a sexual encounter with Person B. Person A immediately kills Person B. Person A may be guilty of voluntary manslaughter instead of murder.*

**EXAMPLE**

*Person A finds Person A's girlfriend in a sexual encounter with Person B. Person A leaves the house and goes to watch TV at a friend's house. When Person A returns home, Person A shoots and kills Person B. Person A is guilty of murder, not voluntary manslaughter.*

*Type of crime:* Felony

*Punishment:* 1 to 20 years imprisonment

## 📢 Pay Attention!

**Voluntary manslaughter is one of the seven deadly sins. A person 13-16 years old when the crime was committed can be prosecuted and punished as an adult for the crime of voluntary manslaughter.**

# CHAPTER TWENTY-TWO
## *SELF-DEFENSE*

People often ask when self-defense is appropriate and what kind of self-defense is legal. My first advice is to try to avoid the issue. If at all possible, remove yourself from the situation. There are worse things than being called a coward, such as death or prison.

If self-defense is absolutely necessary to protect yourself, you cannot use deadly force, for example a gun, unless deadly force is being threatened against you.

**Self-defense** may be a legal defense for certain crimes.

If a person uses force or threatens to use force against you, you may use self-defense if you reasonably believe that force, and the degree of force that you use, is necessary to defend yourself or a third person from immediate harm.

You may only use <u>deadly force</u> or force that is likely to cause serious bodily injury if you reasonably believe that such force is necessary to prevent death or serious bodily injury to yourself or a third person. Deadly force or force that may cause serious bodily injury is also permissible to prevent a forcible felony.

**EXAMPLE**

*Person B is threatening Person A with a knife. Person A reasonably believes that Person B is about to kill or seriously injure Person A. Person A is justified in shooting Person B to prevent injury to Person A.*

**EXAMPLE**

*Person B is forcibly trying to have sex with Person A against Person A's will. Person A believes that Person B is about to rape her. Person A may kill or seriously injure Person B in self-defense.*

A person is not required to retreat before using force to defend the person or a third person.

In some situations, self-defense will not be a valid legal defense for using force against another person. You may not use force:

- If you are the initial aggressor *or* were engaged in a fight by mutual agreement
- If you provoke force against another person with the intent of inflicting bodily harm

**EXAMPLE**

*Person A picks a fight with Person B. When Person B retaliates, Person A uses force against Person B, which causes Person B to have a broken nose. Person A cannot use self-defense as a defense for Person A's actions.*

# CHAPTER TWENTY-THREE
## *STEALING*

## SHOPLIFTING

*Two young women entered an upscale department store in a mall. They both were carrying bags containing purchases from other stores. They believed no one was watching them, and they placed several expensive items in their bags and exited the store without paying for the merchandise. They were immediately apprehended by store security and arrested for shoplifting. Their theft was recorded on high definition digital recording. The recording was so clear you could read the numbers on the price tags! Both women were charged with the felony crime of shoplifting.*

Most establishments today have high technological surveillance equipment that allows store personnel to observe and record a shopper's every move. Just because you do not see anyone does not mean "Big Brother" is not watching.

(i) *The crime of shoplifting occurs when a person:*
- *Conceals or takes possession of the merchandise of any store or retail establishment with the intent to take the merchandise without paying for the merchandise*
- *Alters the price tag or other pricing so as to reflect a lesser price than the actual price*

- *Swaps the price tag from one item to another item to lower the price of the purchased item*
- *Conceals the merchandise by placing it inside another container*
- *Wrongfully causes the amount to be paid to be less than the actual price*

*Type of crime: Misdemeanor* if the retail value of the merchandise shoplifted is $300.00 or less; *felony* if the retail value of the merchandise shoplifted is more than $300.00
*Punishment:* 1 to 10 years imprisonment for *felony*; up to 12 months imprisonment for *misdemeanor*

> **EXAMPLE**
> *Person A changes the price tag on a jacket from $350.00 to $250.00, goes to the cash register, and pays $250.00 for the jacket. Person A is guilty of felony shoplifting because the retail value of the item is more than $300.00.*

## THEFT BY TAKING

The crime of theft by taking occurs when a person:
- *Takes property of another person without that person's consent*
- *Keeps the property of another person without the intention of returning the property to its rightful owner*

*Type of crime: Misdemeanor* if the property has a value of $500 or less; *felony* if the property has a value of more than $500

*Punishment:* 1 to 10 years imprisonment for *felony*; up to 12 months imprisonment for *misdemeanor*

✕ **Exception:** The judge has discretion to treat a felony as a misdemeanor.

✕ **Exception:** Theft of a motor vehicle of any value, or theft of a motor vehicle part worth more than $100 is a felony.

✕ **Exception:** Theft of a firearm of any value is a felony.

> ***EXAMPLE***
> *Person A steals the hubcaps and rims of a car belonging to Person B. The total value of the car parts stolen is more than $100. Person A is guilty of felony theft by taking.*

## THEFT BY RECEIVING STOLEN PROPERTY

Teenagers can get in serious trouble for being in possession of something they had no idea was stolen, usually a car. This is where common sense should take control. If you are not absolutely sure that the rightful owner of a vehicle has given you permission to drive the car, don't get behind the wheel.

(i) *The crime of theft by receiving stolen property occurs when a person receives, disposes, retains, or keeps stolen property that the person knows is stolen property or should know is stolen property.*

✗ **Exception:** The person has the property because the person intends to give it back to the rightful owner.

*EXAMPLE*
*Person B loans a car to Person A. Person A has never seen the car before. Person B did not tell Person A where Person B got the car. Person A notices that the ignition lock on the car is broken and must be started with a screwdriver. Person A drives the car. Under these facts, Person A should know that the car is probably stolen. Person A can be charged with theft by receiving stolen property.*

*EXAMPLE*
*Person A finds a wallet in some bushes that appears to have been stolen. Person A tries to contact the owner of the wallet. Person A is not guilty of theft by receiving stolen property.*

*Type of crime: Misdemeanor* if the property has a value of $500 or less; *felony* if the property has a value of more than $500

*Punishment:* 1 to 10 years imprisonment for *felony*; up to 12 months imprisonment for *misdemeanor*

✗ **Exception:** The judge has discretion to treat a felony as a misdemeanor.

✗ **Exception:** Receiving a stolen motor vehicle of any value, or receiving a stolen motor vehicle part worth more than $100 is a felony.

✗ **Exception:** Receiving a stolen firearm of any value is a felony.

# CHAPTER TWENTY-FOUR
## *INVADING ANOTHER PERSON'S PROPERTY*

## CRIMINAL TRESPASS

### ♀ *Did You Know?*
**DID YOU KNOW that throwing toilet paper in someone's yard is a crime?**

Fortunately, most people whose yards are rolled just call the culprits if they know them and have them come clean up the mess. However, if the homeowner wants to press charges, the homeowner can insist that the persons who threw the toilet paper be arrested for criminal trespass.

(i) *The crime of criminal trespass occurs when a person:*
- *Intentionally damages the property of another person without the other person's consent, and the damage is not more than $500.00*
- *Knowingly and without permission enters upon the property, motor vehicle, aircraft, or boat of another to commit a crime*
- *After being notified that entry is forbidden, either in person or by a posted sign from the owner, enters upon the owner's property, motor vehicle, aircraft, or boat*
- *After being notified to leave by the owner or a person*

*representing the owner, remains on the owner's proper-
ty, motor vehicle, aircraft, or boat*
- *Defaces, mutilates, or defiles a grave marker or monu-
ment to a veteran*

### EXAMPLE

*A "No Trespassing" sign is posted on Person B's property in
several visible locations. Person A uses Person B's property
as a shortcut between his house and a friend's house. Person
A is guilty of criminal trespass.*

*Type of crime:* Misdemeanor
*Punishment:* Up to 12 months imprisonment

## CRIMINAL DAMAGE TO PROPERTY

*Two teenagers set fires in churches when they were not occupied.
They were arrested and charged with criminal damage to property in the second degree. The teenagers would have been charged
with criminal damage to property in the first degree if anyone
had been inside a church when the fire was ignited.*

(i) **The crime of criminal damage to property in the first
degree occurs if a person knowingly and without
authority interferes with any property so as to endanger
human life.**

*Type of crime:* Felony
*Punishment:* 1 to 10 years imprisonment

 **The crime of criminal damage to property in the second degree occurs if a person:**

- **Intentionally damages the property of another person, and the damage to the property exceeds $500.00**
- **Intentionally or recklessly damages another person's property by fire or explosives**
- **Starts a fire on another's land without consent, with the intent to damage property**

### EXAMPLE

*Person A slashes all four tires of Person B's new car. The cost to replace the tires exceeds $500.00. Person A is guilty of felony criminal damage to property in the second degree.*

### EXAMPLE

*Person A builds a fire on Person A's property to burn some trash. The fire is very close to Person B's house. The fire gets out of control and burns Person B's house. Person A is guilty of criminal damage to property in the second degree.*

## ◀»» Pay Attention!

**"Spinning doughnuts" in a car on a lawn may seem like just a prank, but the cost of repair will almost certainly be over $500, and the prank will then be a felony.**

*Type of Crime*:  Felony
*Punishment*:  1 to 5 years imprisonment

## VANDALISM TO A PLACE OF WORSHIP

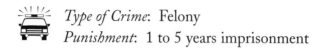 **Did You Know?**

**DID YOU KNOW that it is a felony to vandalize, paint graffiti, or in any manner intentionally harm a place of worship?**

*A teenager painted a swastika on a synagogue. The teenager was arrested and charged with the felony crime of vandalism of a place of worship.*

**(i)** **A crime occurs when a person intentionally damages a church, synagogue, mosque, or other place of worship. The extent of damage or cost of repair does not matter.**

*Type of Crime*:  Felony
*Punishment*:  1 to 5 years in prison

## BURGLARY

**(i)** **The crime of burglary occurs when a person, without authority or permission, enters or remains within a**

*dwelling house of another or any other building, railroad car, or aircraft, for the purpose of committing a theft (of any amount) or other felony.*

A "dwelling house" includes any building, vehicle, railroad car, watercraft, or other structure designed as a dwelling of another.

*Type of crime:* Felony
*Punishment:* 1 to 20 years imprisonment

## REMAINING IN A SCHOOL SAFETY ZONE WITHOUT A REASON

(i) *The crime of remaining in a school safety zone without a reason occurs when a person remains upon school premises or within 1000 feet of a school after being asked by a school official to leave or fails to check in at a designated location.*

"School" means a public or private elementary school, middle school, high school, technical school, vocational school, college, university, or institution of post-secondary education.

*Type of crime:* Misdemeanor
*Punishment:* Up to 12 months imprisonment

# CHAPTER TWENTY-FIVE
## *CRIMINAL STREET GANG*

The Criminal Street Gang law is a tool used by police and prosecutors to break up gangs and punish people who associate together to commit crimes. While punishment for the original crime might not be that severe, if the crime is done as part of gang activity, the punishment can be very harsh.

##  *Did You Know?*

**DID YOU KNOW that if you write graffiti on a building that causes damage of less than $500, you can receive up to 1 year in prison? HOWEVER, if you write graffiti on a building as a member of a gang, you can receive up to 16 years in prison if you are 17 years old or older?**

ⓘ **The crimes related to criminal street gangs occur when a person:**

- **Is associated with a criminal street gang and participates in criminal gang activity**
- **Encourages, solicits, or coerces another person to participate in a criminal street gang**
- **Threatens another person or a member of the other person's family so as to deter the other person from withdrawing from a criminal street gang**

Criminal street gang means an organization, association, or group of three or more people that engages in "criminal gang activity." The group can be formal with a name, symbol, and officers or an informal loose association.

The following evidence can be used to prove the existence of a gang: name, identifying signs, symbols, tattoos, graffiti, clothing, or other distinguishing characteristics.

(i) **Criminal gang activity occurs when a person commits, attempts to commit, solicits another person to commit, or intimidates another person to commit crimes, such as:**
- **Any crime that involves violence, such as aggravated assault or battery**
- **Any crime that involves possession of a weapon, such as possession of a pistol, revolver, or metal knuckles**
- **Any crime that involves the use of a weapon**
- **Stalking**
- **Rape**
- **Aggravated sodomy**
- **Statutory rape**
- **Aggravated sexual battery**
- **Criminal trespass or criminal damage to property that is the result of marking on, writing on, or creating graffiti on the property of another**
- **Furnishing metal knuckles or a knife to a person under 18 years old**
- **Furnishing a pistol or a revolver to a person under 18 years old**

- *Pointing a pistol at another person*
- *Discharging a gun near a public highway or street*
- *Possession of a sawed-off shotgun or rifle*

*This list of crimes is representative and not all-inclusive.*

*Type of crime:* Felony
*Punishment:* 1 to 15 years imprisonment in addition to punishment for the underlying crime(s).

---

**EXAMPLE**

*Person A, Person B, and Person C are all 17 years old and are associated with a criminal street gang. Person A and Person B encourage Person C to have consensual sex with a 15 year old girl. Person C can receive up to 1 year in prison for misdemeanor statutory rape, plus Person A, Person B, and Person C can receive up to 15 years in prison for participating in and/or encouraging criminal gang activity.*

# CHAPTER TWENTY-SIX
## WEAPONS AND FIREARMS

## POSSESSION OF A PISTOL OR REVOLVER

As a result of the increased wave of violence by teenagers, most states have passed strict laws prohibiting the possession of a pistol or revolver by anyone under 18 years old, except in very limited situations. A minor who possesses a pistol or revolver is guilty of a misdemeanor; a person who gives a minor a pistol or revolver is guilty of a felony, except in limited situations.

(i) *A crime occurs when a person under 18 years old possesses a pistol or revolver.*

✗ **Exceptions:** A person under 18 years old may possess a pistol or revolver if the person is in any of the following situations:
- Attending a hunter education course or a firearms safety course
- Engaging in target practice at a shooting range authorized by the county or city
- Engaging in an organized competition involving the use of a firearm or practicing with such organization, and the organization is sanctioned for such purpose by the federal government

- Hunting or fishing with a valid hunting or fishing license, has the license in the person's possession, has permission of the land owner to hunt or fish on the property, and the pistol or revolver is fully exposed to view
- Permitted by a parent or guardian to possess a pistol or revolver on the land of the parent or guardian
- Permitted by the parent or guardian to possess a pistol or revolver for the purpose of defending the person or others from serious bodily harm at the residence of the parent or guardian

*Type of crime:* Misdemeanor
*Punishment:* Up to 12 months imprisonment

While traveling to the activities described in the first four exceptions described above, the pistol or revolver must be unloaded.

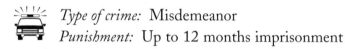

## SELLING OR FURNISHING A PISTOL TO A PERSON UNDER 18 YEARS OLD

ⓘ *A crime occurs when a person intentionally, know-ingly, or recklessly sells or furnishes a pistol or revolver to a person under 18 years old.*

**✕ Exceptions:** A parent or guardian of a person under 18 years old may allow the person to possess a weapon if the person is in any of the following situations:

- Attending a hunter education course or a firearms safety course
- Engaging in target practice at a shooting range authorized by the county or city
- Engaging in an organized competition involving the use of a firearm or practicing with such organization, and the organization is sanctioned for such purpose by the federal government
- Hunting or fishing with a valid hunting or fishing license, has the license in the person's possession, has permission of the land owner to hunt or fish on the property, and the pistol or revolver is fully exposed to view
- Permitted by a parent or guardian to possess a pistol or revolver on the land of the parent or guardian
- Permitted by the parent or guardian to possess a pistol or revolver for the purpose of defending the person or others from serious bodily harm at the residence of the parent or guardian

 *Type of crime:* Felony
*Punishment:* 3 to 5 years imprisonment

## METAL KNUCKLES AND KNIVES

(i) *A crime occurs when a person knowingly sells or furnishes metal knuckles or a knife that is used for the purpose of "offense or defense" to a person under 18 years old.*

Whether a knife is used for the purpose of "offense or defense" (in other words, as a weapon) is usually a question for a jury to determine. Some knives are obviously not for use as a weapon, such as a scouting knife. Other knives may be questionable, such as a large hunting knife. Important factors to consider are where, when, and how the knife was given to a person under 18 years old.

 *Type of crime:* Misdemeanor
*Punishment:* Up to 12 months imprisonment

## POSSESSION OF A WEAPON IN A SCHOOL SAFETY ZONE

(i) *A crime occurs when a person possesses, or has within the person's control, a weapon or explosive device within 1000 feet of a public or private elementary school, middle school, high school, technical school, vocational school, college, university, institution of post-secondary education, school bus, school function, or school property.*

A <u>weapon</u> includes a pistol, revolver, dirk, bowie knife, switchblade, or any knife having a blade greater than 2 inches, metal knuckles, blackjack, throwing star, stun gun, taser, razors, bats, or clubs, unless authorized for academic or athletic purposes.

The fact that the weapon or explosive device is locked in a person's vehicle is no defense.

> **EXAMPLE**
> *Person A drives Person A's car to school and has a knife with a blade longer then 2 inches in the glove compartment. Person A is guilty of unlawful possession of a weapon in a school safety zone.*

*Type of crime:* Felony
*Punishment:* 2 to 10 years imprisonment

## ◀)) *Pay Attention!*

**If the weapon is a firearm, the punishment is 5 to 10 years imprisonment**

**ⓘ** **The crime of gambling occurs when a person engages in any of the following activities:**

- **Plays and bets for money or anything else of value at any game played with cards, dice or balls**
- **Makes a bet on the partial or final outcome of a game**
- **Makes a bet on the performance of an individual in a game**

> **EXAMPLE**
>
> *Person A and three of Person A's friends play a card game of Texas Hold 'Em, and they each buy poker chips to use in the game. All four persons are guilty of the crime of gambling.*
>
> **EXAMPLE**
>
> *Person A places a bet that the Falcons will win the division championship. Person A is guilty of gambling.*
>
> **EXAMPLE**
>
> *Person A places a bet on how many yards a quarterback will throw in a football game. Person A is guilty of gambling.*

*Type of crime:* Misdemeanor
*Punishment:* Up to 12 months imprisonment

# III

## EXTRA STUFF

# CHAPTER TWENTY-EIGHT
## *DRIVING CARS AND BOATS*

## LEARNER'S DRIVING PERMIT
## [CLASS P INSTRUCTION PERMIT]

<u>Requirements for obtaining a learner's permit (Class P Instruction Permit):</u>

You must be at least 15 years old to qualify for a Class P permit.

✗ **Exception:** If you are under 16 years old and have been convicted of possession of marijuana, possession of a controlled substance, possession of a dangerous drug, or driving under the influence of alcohol or drugs, you cannot apply for a learner's permit or driver's license until your 17th birthday.

**When you go to the Department of Driver Services to apply for a learner's permit:**

- You must take your original birth certificate or a certified copy of your birth certificate, or a valid passport.
- You must know your social security number.
- You must have your parent or legal guardian go with you.

- You must take a notarized Georgia Department of Driver Services Certificate of Attendance form signed by a school official within 30 days of your application. (If you are under 18 years old and are not enrolled in school, you must provide a (i) GED diploma, (ii) a high school diploma, or (iii) an attendance form from your local board of education showing enrollment in an approved home school program.)

### At the Department of Driver Services:
- You must pass an eye test.
- You must pass a written examination regarding knowledge of the "Georgia Driver's Manual."
- You must pay a $10 (cash) license fee.

With a learner's permit, you must always drive with a passenger who is at least 21 years old, has a valid driver's license, and is not under the influence of alcohol or drugs.

## ♀ *Did You Know?*
**DID YOU KNOW that if you have a learner's permit, you cannot be the designated driver for your adult passenger who has been drinking or using drugs?**

For more information on obtaining a learner's permit, you may go to the Department of Driver Services website (www.dds.ga.gov).

# DRIVER'S LICENSE (CLASS D DRIVER'S LICENSE)

## Requirements for obtaining a driver's license (Class D Driver's License):

### To qualify for a Class D Driver's License in Georgia:

- You must be at least 16 years old.
- You must have had a valid learner's permit for 12 consecutive months + 1 day without suspension.
- You must have less than four driving points on your record.
- You must be a resident of Georgia.
- You must have successfully completed a driver education course approved by the Department of Driver Services.
- You must have completed 40 hours of supervised driving with a parent or legal guardian who has a valid driver's license, including 6 hours at night.

To avoid a long wait, make an appointment to take the driving test with the Department of Driver Services. You can call to make an appointment up to 90 days in advance.

## When you go to the Department of Driver Services to apply for a Class D Driver's License:

- You must have a parent or legal guardian go with you to provide sworn verification that you have completed at least 40 hours of on-the-road driving, including at least 6 hours of night driving.
- You must take a signed card showing completion of the Alcohol and Drug Awareness Program.
- You must know your social security number.
- You must take a notarized Georgia Department of Driver Services Certificate of Attendance form signed by a school official within 30 days of application. (If you are under 18 years old and are not enrolled in school, you must provide a (i) GED diploma, or (ii) high school diploma, or (iii) attendance form from your local board of education showing enrollment in an approved home school program.)

## At the Department of Driver Services:

- You must pass an eye examination.
- You must take a driving test.
- You must provide a car for the driving test that has a valid tag and valid proof of insurance (the car cannot be a rental car and must pass a safety inspection).
- You must pay the $10.00 (cash) license fee.

For more information on obtaining a driver's license, you may go to the Department of Driver Services website (www.dds.ga.gov).

## DRIVING RESTRICTIONS FOR PERSONS 16 AND 17 YEARS OLD (CLASS D DRIVER'S LICENSE)

**If you have a Class D Driver's License:**
- You may not drive between midnight and 6:00 a.m. There are no exceptions, including school sponsored events and employment.
- You may not drive with anyone but a member of your immediate family for the first 6 months after receiving your driver's license.
- After the first 6 months, you may not drive with more than 1 passenger under 21 years old who is not a member of your immediate family.
- After the second 6 months and for the duration of your Class D license, you may not drive with more then 3 passengers under 21 years old who are not members of your immediate family.

A violation of one of these restrictions can only be a secondary offense. That means you can only be charged with a violation of one of these restrictions if you are charged with another offense, such as speeding, running a red light, having a tail light out, or having an expired tag.

> **EXAMPLE**
> *Person A is caught speeding after midnight, and Person A is 17 years old with a Class D Driver's License. Person A can be charged both with speeding and violating the law which prohibits persons with Class D Driver's Licenses from driving after midnight.*

## FULL LICENSE FOR PERSONS 18 YEARS OLD OR OLDER (CLASS C DRIVER'S LICENSE)

When you turn 18 years old, you are eligible to receive a Class C Driver's License:

1. If you have not been convicted of any of the crimes listed below during the preceding 12 months:
   - hit-and-run
   - reckless driving
   - drag racing
   - eluding a police officer
   - driving under the influence of drugs or alcohol
   - any traffic citation that assesses 4 or more points
2. If you have not accumulated 4 or more driving points during the previous 12 months.

When you turn 18 years old, remember to apply for a Class C Driver's License with the Department of Driver Services. Otherwise, you will continue to be held to the restrictions of the Class D Driver's License.

### ◀))  *Pay Attention!*

*Always have your learner's permit or driver's license, proof of insurance, and car registration when you drive. This applies when you are driving any car, even cars that do not belong to you or your family.*

## WHAT TO DO IF YOU ARE IN A CAR ACCIDENT

If you are in an accident on a public highway or street, you must stop at the scene of the accident and call the police and report the accident. If the accident occurs on private property, such as a driveway or parking lot, and no one is injured, you must still stop at the scene of the accident, but you do not have to notify the police.

You need to exchange names, addresses, phone numbers, driver's license number, license plate number, make and model of car, and insurance information with the other driver any time you are involved in an accident.

## BOATING AND PERSONAL WATERCRAFT (JET SKIS)

**Requirements for persons 16 years old and older (boats and personal watercraft):** If you are 16 years old or older, you may operate any boat or personal watercraft (such as a jet ski), with proper identification showing your age. You do not need to have a learner's permit or driver's license for a car to operate a motor boat or a jet ski.

**Requirements for persons 14 and 15 years old (boats):** If you are 14 or 15 years old, you may operate any boat under one of the following conditions:

- If you are accompanied by an adult 18 years old or older, and the adult has proper identification
- If you are under the direct supervision of an adult 18 years old or older
- If you have completed and have proof of completion of a boating course approved by the Department of Natural Resources

**Requirements for persons 12 to 15 years old (personal watercraft):** If you are 12 to 15 years old, you may operate a personal watercraft (such as a jet ski) under one of the following conditions:

- If an adult 18 years old or older is on the jet ski with you, and the adult has proper identification
- If you are under the direct supervision of an adult 18 years old or older
- If you have successfully completed and have proof of completion of a personal watercraft safety program approved by the Department of Natural Resources

Direct supervision means that the adult is within 400 yards and within sight of the minor, and the adult is aware of responsibility for the minor. For example, if you are 14 or 15 years old, you may drive a ski boat pulling a skier who is 18 years old.

An adult accompanying or supervising a minor cannot be under the influence of alcohol or drugs.

**Other requirements for jet skis regardless of age:**

- You may not drive a jet ski after sunset or before sunrise.
- You must always drive or ride a jet ski with a proper life jacket.
- No one who owns or has charge of a jet ski may authorize or knowingly allow a person under 16 years old to violate the laws regarding jet skis.

# CHAPTER TWENTY-NINE
## *OTHER GENERAL LAWS OF INTEREST*

When I speak to groups of teenagers regarding Georgia law, they often ask questions about topics unrelated to criminal matters. You may have similar questions. The following are some general topics of interest to teenagers.

## ABORTION

If you are at least 18 years old, you can legally get an abortion without your parent's knowledge or consent. If you are under 18 years old, unmarried, and still under your parent's care and control, then an abortion may only proceed under very limited circumstances. If you are under 18 years old and are seeking an abortion without your parent's or guardian's knowledge or consent, you need to contact the local juvenile court for information.

## ARMED SERVICES AND REGISTRATION FOR THE DRAFT

If you are 17 years old, you may join the military with the permission of a parent. If you are 18 years old, you may join the military without the consent of a parent.

Every male who is a United States citizen and most resident alien males must register for the draft when they turn 18 years old. You may receive a registration form in the mail, or you can find more information online at www.sss.gov.

## BODY PIERCING

### ♀ *Did You Know?*

*DID YOU KNOW that if you are under 18 years old, your parent or guardian must consent in writing to the piercing of any body part other than your ear lobes?*

A person who pierces the body (except for the ear lobes) of any person under 18 years old for the purpose of inserting jewelry or similar objects into the body commits a misdemeanor unless the person under 18 years old has prior written consent of a custodial parent or guardian.

## CELL PHONES IN SCHOOLS

You are not allowed to use cell phones, pagers, or other communication devices during classroom instruction time in primary and secondary schools.

Local school boards can establish rules and penalties regarding possession of cell phones, pagers, and other communication devices on school property.

## CHOOSING TO LIVE WITH A DIVORCED PARENT

If you are 14 years old or older, you can decide which parent you want to reside with if your parents are divorced.

## EMANCIPATED MINOR

After you are 16 years old, you may become <u>emancipated</u> – no longer under the control and supervision of a parent – by one of the following methods:
- Entering into a valid marriage
- Reaching 18 years old
- Being on active duty in the military
- Having a court order from a juvenile court judge

An emancipated minor has the same rights as an adult *except* that an emancipated minor must still be 18 years old to vote and 21 years old to possess/consume alcoholic beverages.

## MARRIAGE

### ♀ *Did You Know?*

**DID YOU KNOW that you must be at least 18 years old before entering into marriage without your parent's consent?**

If you are 16 or 17 years old, you may get married with your parent's consent.

## TATTOOING

### ♀ *Did You Know?*

**DID YOU KNOW that you cannot lawfully get a tattoo from a non-medical person until you are 18 years old? A person who tattoos the body of any person under 18 years old commits a misdemeanor unless the person is a licensed physician or an osteopath.**

## TOBACCO

If you are under 18 years old, you may not purchase, attempt to purchase, or possess cigarettes or tobacco related objects (such as chewing tobacco), unless you are in the presence of your own home, and the cigarettes or tobacco are given to you by your parents.

This violation is neither a misdemeanor nor a felony. The punishment for this violation is 20 hours of community service and/or attendance of a lecture on the hazards of smoking.

## UNRULY CHILD/LOITERING

## ♀ *Did You Know?*

*DID YOU KNOW that you are an "unruly child" if you are under 17 years old and are hanging out on a street or in a public place between the hours of midnight and 5:00 a.m.?*

An "unruly child" is a person under 17 years old who:
- Is absent from school on a regular basis without a legitimate excuse
- Is a runaway from home
- Disobeys reasonable commands from a parent

- Wanders or loiters about the streets of any city or highways or any other public place between the hours of midnight and 5:00 a.m.
- Goes to a bar without a parent or possesses alcohol

The juvenile court judge determines if you are an "unruly child."

# AGE OF RESPONSIBILITY CHART

| 12 | 13 | 14 | 15 |
|---|---|---|---|
| Can operate a jet ski under certain conditions | Can be prosecuted as an adult for certain crimes | Can choose which divorced parent to reside with; may operate a motor boat under certain conditions | Can obtain a learner's permit |

| 16 | 17 | 18 | 21 |
|---|---|---|---|
| Can obtain a restricted driver's license; can consent to sexual contact | Must be prosecuted as an adult for all crimes | Must register for draft; can vote; serve alcohol in a restaurant; possess unrestricted driver's license; marry; get an abortion without parental consent; join military; be emancipated from parents | May consume & possess alcohol |

# GLOSSARY

## DEFINITION OF CERTAIN LEGAL TERMS AS USED IN THIS BOOK

**Adjudication of Delinquency:** a ruling by a juvenile court judge that a person under 17 years old has committed an act that would be a crime if the person were 17 years old or older

**Age of prosecution as adult:** the age at which a person will be prosecuted as an adult, which is 17 years old in Georgia

**Age of consent:** the legal age for consent to sexual contact, which is 16 years old in Georgia

**Arrest:** the taking of a person into custody against the person's will for the purpose of criminal prosecution or interrogation

**Confinement:** sentence given to a person convicted of a crime to be served in a prison or jail; also called incarceration or imprisonment; often used to refer to a sentence given to a delinquent child to be served in a juvenile detention facility

**Crime:** an act of doing something that violates written law which may be punished with imprisonment

**Custody:** detention of a person in a situation in which a reasonable person does not feel free to leave

**Defendant**: person who is charged with committing a crime; also called offender or perpetrator

**Delinquent Act**: an act committed by a person under 17 years old that would be a crime if committed by a person 17 years old or older

**Delinquent Child**: person under 17 years old who has committed a delinquent act and is in need of treatment or rehabilitation

**Deprived child**: person under 17 years old who does not receive adequate sustenance, care, or supervision

**Designated Felony Act**: crime for which a person 13, 14, 15, or 16 years old can be sentenced up to 5 years in confinement by the juvenile court judge

**District Attorney**: the elected attorney who oversees the prosecution of felonies in one or more counties and, in smaller counties, oversees the prosecution of misdemeanors

**Emancipated Minor**: a person under 18 years old who is no longer under the control of a parent or guardian, usually as the result of a court order or marriage

**Felony**: crime for which the punishment is more than 12 months in prison, life imprisonment, or death

**Fine**: money required to be paid as punishment for violation of a law or ordinance

**Frisk:** pat-down of outer clothing performed by a police officer if the police officer has a reasonable suspicion that criminal activity has just taken place or is about to take place and reason to believe that a person is armed and dangerous

**Guilt beyond a Reasonable Doubt:** standard of proof that a prosecutor must satisfy in order to prove a person committed a crime

**Imprisonment:** sentence given to a person convicted of a crime to be served in a prison or jail; also called incarceration or confinement

**Incarceration:** sentence given to a person convicted of a crime to be served in a prison or jail; also called imprisonment or confinement

**Juvenile:** person under 17 years old in Georgia

**Juvenile Court:** court in Georgia which has jurisdiction and control over most legal issues involving persons under 17 years old

**Juvenile Detention Facility:** place where juvenile offenders serve a sentence of confinement

**Minor:** person who has not yet reached legal age; in Georgia, a person reaches legal age at 17, 18, or 21 years old, depending on the circumstances

**Miranda Warnings:** cautionary instructions which law enforcement must give a person in custody before interrogation

**Misdemeanor:** crime for which the punishment is 12 months or less in prison

**Offender:** person who is charged with committing a crime or violation of law; also called defendant or perpetrator

**Official Code of Georgia Annotated:** the complete set of statutes enacted by the state legislature in Georgia

**Ordinance:** law passed by the governing authority of a city or county

**Parole:** early release from prison

**Parties to a Crime:** all persons involved in committing, planning, participating, helping, advising, encouraging, or benefiting in a criminal activity

**Perpetrator:** person who is charged with committing a crime or violation of law; also called defendant or offender

**Probable Cause:** the belief of a reasonable person that a crime has been committed or that evidence of a crime is at a particular location; probable cause is more than reasonable suspicion but less than proof of guilt beyond a reasonable doubt

**Probation:** punishment for a violation of law served outside of prison with certain conditions, restrictions, and requirements

**Prosecution:** the process of charging and proving that a person committed a crime beyond a reasonable doubt

**Prosecutor:** the person who handles the prosecution of a crime against a defendant

**Proximate Cause:** an act or omission that directly causes something to occur

**Reasonable Suspicion:** belief of a reasonable person that is based on more than a hunch but less than probable cause that criminal activity has just taken place or is about to take place

**School Official:** a person in a position of authority in a school, such as a teacher or principal

**School Resource Officer:** a law enforcement official assigned to a school who is either employed by the school system or the local police department

**Search Warrant:** a document obtained by a law enforcement official upon proof to a judge of probable cause to conduct a search of a person or property

**Self-incrimination:** the act of saying or doing something that will cause you to appear guilty of a crime

**Sentence:** punishment issued by a judge (or jury in a death penalty case) to a person who is guilty of committing a crime or delinquent act

**Seven Deadly Sins:** seven serious crimes for which persons 13, 14, 15, and 16 years old can be prosecuted and punished as an adult (murder/felony murder, voluntary manslaughter, rape, aggravated sodomy, aggravated child molestation, aggravated sexual battery, and robbery with a firearm)

**Sexual Contact:** any type of sexual activity, including touching of the other person's breasts or sexual organs or buttocks, oral sex, or sexual intercourse

**Solicitor-General:** the elected attorney in larger counties in Georgia who oversees the prosecution of misdemeanors in state court

**State Court:** the court in larger counties in Georgia which has jurisdiction over misdemeanors

**State Legislature:** the governing body of Georgia consisting of two bodies (the House of Representatives and the Senate) elected by the people which enacts written laws

**Statute:** written law enacted by the state legislature which is included in the *Official Code of Georgia Annotated*

**Summons:** an order for you to appear in court on a specific date and at a specific time

**Superior Court:** the court in Georgia which has jurisdiction over felonies and, in counties which do not have state courts, has jurisdiction over misdemeanors

**Sustenance:** necessary food or drink sufficient to support life and maintain health

**United States Constitution:** the supreme law of the United States, which includes Amendments, such as the Fourth, Fifth, and Sixth Amendments

**United States Supreme Court:** the highest court in the United States which reviews cases decided by other courts and interprets questions about the United States Constitution

**Unruly child:** a person under 17 years old who is absent from school on a regular basis without a legitimate excuse; is a runaway from home; disobeys reasonable commands from a parent; wanders or loiters about the streets of any city or highways or any other public place between the hours of midnight and 5:00 a.m.; or goes to a bar without a parent or possesses alcohol

**Victim:** a person against whom a crime is committed

**Written law:** a rule or requirement set forth in writing

# INDEX

# APPENDIX

## *CITATIONS OF STATUTES*

If you wish to find the actual wording of a particular statute, you may use the citations found below. "O.C.G.A." stands for *The Official Code of Georgia Annotated*, and the numbers following the symbol (§) reference the statute. *The Official Code of Georgia Annotated* is available on-line at the following website: http://www.lexis-nexis.com/hottopics/gacode/default.asp. Type in the number of the statute you wish to read, and the most current version of the law will appear on the screen.

### *FUNDAMENTALS*

CHAPTER ONE: CRIME AND PUNISHMENT
   Types of Crimes and Punishment : O.C.G.A. §§ 16-1-3, 15-10-60, 15-11-2

CHAPTER THREE: YOUR RIGHTS AS A
   TEENAGER: ARRESTS
   Fingerprinting and Photographing a Person Under 17 Years Old Who is Charged with a Crime:  O.C.G.A. § 15-11-83

CHAPTER FOUR: PARTIES TO A CRIME
   (WHO CAN BE CHARGED WITH A CRIME):
   O.C.G.A. §16-2-20

# WHAT'S THE CRIME?

## *DRUGS AND ALCOHOL*

ID to Purchase Alcohol: O.C.G.A. §§ 16-9-4, 3-3-23, 3-3-23.1
Making, Selling, or Distributing False Identification: O.C.G.A. § 16-9-4

CHAPTER TEN: POSSESSION AND SALE OF MARIJUANA: O.C.G.A § 16-13-30

CHAPTER ELEVEN: POSSESSION AND SALE OF OTHER ILLEGAL DRUGS OR LEGAL DRUGS WITHOUT A PRESCRIPTION: O.C.G.A § 16-13-20 et. seq.

CHAPTER TWELVE: OTHER DRUG-RELATED LAWS
Asking a Person Under 17 Years Old to Deliver Illegal Drugs: O.C.G.A. § 16-13-30
Inhalation of Model Glue: O.C.G.A § 16-13-91
Possession of Drug Related Object: O.C.G.A. § 16-13-32.2
Illegal Drugs in a School Safety Zone: O.C.G.A. § 16-13-32.4
Illegal Drugs near a Park or Public Housing Project: O.C.G.A. § 16-13-32.5
Manufacture, Distribution, or Possession of Fake Illegal Drugs: O.C.G.A. § 16-13-78.2
First Offense for Possession of Illegal Drugs: O.C.G.A. § 16-13-2

### *SEX CRIMES*

CHAPTER FIFTEEN: AGE OF CONSENT AND
STATUTORY RAPE: O.C.G.A. § 16-6-3

CHAPTER SIXTEEN: SEX CRIMES WITH FORCE
Rape: O.C.G.A. § 16-6-1
Aggravated Sodomy: O.C.G.A. § 16-6-2
Sexual Battery: O.C.G.A. § 16-6-22.1
Aggravated Sexual Battery: O.C.G.A. § 16-6-22.2

CHAPTER SEVENTEEN: SEX CRIMES AGAINST
CHILDREN
Child Molestation: O.C.G.A. § 16-6-4
Aggravated Child Molestation: O.C.G.A. § 16-6-4(c)
Enticing a Child for Indecent Purposes: O.C.G.A. §
16-6-5
Sexual Assault against a Student by School Officials:
O.C.G.A. § 16-6-5.1
Sexual Exploitation of Persons Under 18 Years Old
(Child Pornography): O.C.G.A. § 16-12-100
Computer Solicitation of Minors for Sex: O.C.G.A. §
16-12-100.2
Reporting Child Abuse: O.C.G.A. § 19-7-5

### *HARM TO PEOPLE*

CHAPTER EIGHTEEN: OTHER CRIMES
AGAINST CHILDREN
Contributing to the Delinquency of a Minor:
O.C.G.A. § 16-12-1

Theft by Receiving Stolen Property: O.C.G.A. § 16-8-7

CHAPTER TWENTY-FOUR: INVADING ANOTH-
ER PERSON'S PROPERTY
Criminal Trespass: O.C.G.A. § 16-7-21
Criminal Damage to Property: O.C.G.A. §§ 16-7-22,
16-7-23
Vandalism to a Place of Worship: O.C.G.A. § 16-7-26
Burglary: O.C.G.A. § 16-7-1
Remaining in a School Safety Zone without a Reason:
O.C.G.A. § 20-2-1180

### *MORE CRIMES*

CHAPTER TWENTY-FIVE: CRIMINAL STREET
GANG: O.C.G.A. §§ 16-15-3, 16-15-4

CHAPTER TWENTY-SIX: WEAPONS AND
FIREARMS
Possession of a Pistol or Revolver: O.C.G.A. § 16-11-132
Selling or Furnishing a Pistol to a Person under 18
Years Old: O.C.G.A. § 16-11-101.1
Metal Knuckles and Knives: O.C.G.A. § 16-11-101
Possession of a Weapon in a School Safety Zone:
O.C.G.A. § 16-11-127.1

CHAPTER TWENTY-SEVEN: OTHER CRIMINAL
LAWS OF INTEREST
Public Indecency: O.C.G.A. § 16-6-8
Gambling: O.C.G.A. § 16-12-21

## *EXTRA STUFF*

## CHAPTER TWENTY-EIGHT: DRIVING CARS AND BOATS

Learner's Driving Permit: O.C.G.A. §§ 40-5-26, 40-5-22

Driver's License: O.C.G.A. § 40-5-24

Driving Restrictions for Persons 16 and 17 Years Old: O.C.G.A. § 40-5-24(2)

Full License for Persons 18 Years Old or Older: O.C.G.A. § 40-5-24(3)

Boating and Personal Watercraft (Jet Skis): O.C.G.A. §§ 52-7-8.2, 52-7-8.3

## CHAPTER TWENTY-NINE: OTHER GENERAL LAWS OF INTEREST

Abortion: O.C.G.A. §§ 15-11-112, 15-11-114

Body Piercing: O.C.G.A. § 16-5-71.1

Cell Phones in Schools: O.C.G.A. § 20-2-1183

Choosing to Live with a Divorced Parent: O.C.G.A. § 19-9-1

Emancipated Minor: O.C.G.A. § 15-11-201

Marriage: O.C.G.A. § 19-3-2

Tattooing: O.C.G.A. § 16-5-71

Tobacco: O.C.G.A. § 16-12-171

Unruly Child/Loitering: O.C.G.A. § 15-11-2(12)(E)

# About the Author

J.Tom Morgan is a nationally rec-
ognized expert on the prosecution
of crimes against children and has
appeared on *CNN*, the *Oprah
Winfrey Show*, *Court TV*, the
*Today Show*, and *48 Hours*. He
served as the District Attorney of
DeKalb County for twelve years
and was the first prosecutor in
Georgia to specialize in the pros-
ecution of crimes against children. Among his numerous
awards, he was the first United States prosecutor to receive
the Special Achievement Award from the International
Association of Prosecutors. J.Tom has dedicated his career
to child advocacy and is committed to helping young people avoid being both victims and perpetrators of crimes.
Currently, he is a trial lawyer in private practice in Decatur,
Georgia specializing in criminal and civil litigation.

A portion of the proceeds of this book will be contributed
to the Georgia Center for Child Advocacy, Inc., a private,
nonprofit organization that provides free treatment for
youth who are victims of abuse.

## TO ORDER THIS BOOK:

Fax or send your purchase order to:
Westchester Legal Press
P.O. Box 1324
Decatur, GA 30031
Fax: (678) 732-9348

### OR

Purchase online at www.ignoranceisnodefense.com

### OR

Call: (678) 732-9348

## FOR SPEAKING ENGAGEMENTS:

Contact J. Tom Morgan at jtom@ignoranceisnodefense.com